TREASURES

A Hunt for the Fine Arts of Living

Mary Ann Sebree • Keitha Kaminski

Westport Publishers, Inc.
Kansas City, Missouri

To Frank
whose unselfish, unlimited
and unstinting confidence, enthusiasm,
patience and support
have made possible Sebree Galleries,
*Le Picnique and **Treasures***

Project Editor: Terry Faulkner
Text and Cover Design: Noelle Kaplan, finedesign
Photography: Harv Gariety and John Perryman
Photo Consultant: Verna Granger
Food Design Consultant: Lon Lane
Room Design Consultant: Joe Haas
Illustrator: Bob Price Holloway

Invaluable assistance, encouragement and understanding by: Mary Louise Orrick, Jean Mongan, Roy Nicodemus, Jeanne Moyer, Linda Brizendine, Melissa Morrow, Barry Barnes, Dawn Williams, Sherry Whitley and Le Picnique staff.

Photos on inside dust jacket as seen in *Distinctively Kansas City* publication

ISBN 0-933701-45-4
Library of Congress Catalog Number 90-050505

Printed in the United States of America

To order additional copies: Westport Publishers, Inc.
4050 Pennsylvania
Kansas City, MO 64111
(800) 347-BOOK

Contents

Preface

Most of us are born treasure hunters. If we're lucky, the childhood fascination with pebbles, shells and terrapins naturally evolves into an adult passion for discovery. Whether pearls, paintings or postage stamps, the objects of the search are often, to the dedicated hunters, less important than the thrill and challenge of the chase itself. For these fortunate folk, each new day — each new place — is super-charged with exciting possibilities...to seek, to find and, perhaps, to have.

The authors of this book hunt for antiques and food...popular pursuits for at least 2,000 years and obsessions of ours. We are twice blessed in that we have been able to turn our obsessions into our business. The purpose of the book is to share our discoveries, particularly in England, France and America, with readers who share our passions. If you're a veteran hunter, our secrets may help to hone your skills. If you're still missing out on some of life's more accessible great adventures, then we invite you to join the chase!

Mary Ann Sebree
Keitha Kaminski
Kansas City, Missouri
1990

Introduction

Sebree Galleries is, coincidentally, the by-product of a treasure hunt. The purchase of a 1920s-Kansas-City-version of a Normandy farmhouse led to a search for appropriate furnishings…which led to an investment in a small antique shop (then Lenord Gallery)…which led to a 22-year learning experience in the extraordinarily challenging and exciting business of finding and bringing to our customers exemplary early furniture, fine arts and decorations from five continents. While we frequently offer 16th century Flemish wood carvings, 17th century Italian paintings and 19th century Chinese porcelains, our focus has always been on 18th century English, French and American furniture. In an age of specialization, even in the antiques trade, we have chosen to remain generalists, thus maximizing our treasure hunting possibilities. In an age of soaring antique prices, we have chosen to make fine quality at reasonable prices our trademark.

Over the years, we have outgrown two shops, but remained on the same block just south of the famous Country Club Plaza, in the cultural heart of Kansas City. To the original antique business, we have added various related services as they were needed: restoration, interior design, appraisals, auctions and estate sales, giving us a legitimate claim to being one of the only "full service" antique shops in the country. Still, a crucial element of antique hunting was missing.

Customers who are seriously considering the purchase of antiques often choose to relax over lunch and a bottle of wine while making their decision. There was no place within walking distance of our shop, even for snacks. To prevent customers from going hungry or…even worse…from going to some other part of the city for such sustenance, we decided to provide an in-house resource for food also. The decision and the reality came together, finally, with the fortuitous arrival of Keitha Kaminski, my co-author, whose consummate chef/manager skills enabled us, in 1981, to open Le Picnique. Originally designed to serve limited light luncheons in an informal picnic style, this quasi-country-French café has expanded to include not only an enlarged menu with full restaurant service for SRO luncheon crowds, but also private parties, catered either in or out of our shop. The success of Keitha (now the manager of our entire operation), her able staff and Le Picnique has been recognized nationally with a coveted award in Mobil guide, but it is still the perfect place for pondering the purchase of a Chippendale chest of drawers.

Our joint experience, Keitha's and mine, in this antiques/food connection, seems to prove beyond doubt that the same perceptive people who treasure authentic antiques feel the same way about quality cuisine...and vice versa. Certainly, hunting for antiques is more fun if you eat along the way. The premise works for us...and we hope it works for you...in your hunt for **treasures**!   *M.A.S.*

Format

There is, of course, historic precedent for the cuisine/decorative arts connection. Evidence indicates that the earliest tribes turned to painting and carving their cave walls as soon as they had plenty to eat. Today the worldwide consumer interest in treasures of the palette and the eye is confirmed on the one hand with a constant flood of new cookbooks, cooking schools, gourmet stores and restaurants and on the other with auction records breaking auction records for antiques and fine arts. The cleverly conceived, created and presented meal, whether classic, nouvelle, regional, ethnic, homecooked or Cordon Bleu, has become the object of a frequent, far-ranging and often expensive search by millions of dedicated food lovers. At the same time, the static supply of antiques in the world has attracted such a horde of well-heeled hunters that prices for great pieces are stratospheric, even modest pieces in good condition are hard to find and fakers have never had such incentive.

So the hunt is on...you're probably part of it or interested in joining it or you would not be reading this book...and we want to provide you with any possible benefit from our professional experience. The problem is to reduce a combined 40 plus years of effort...some successful, some not...into a concise, cohesive and portable volume that does not duplicate information already available. Hundreds of current publications do an excellent job of tracking the world's restaurants and pointing out the "perfect little Left Bank bistro." Our interest is in a contemporary approach to traditional English, French and American menus. If you choose to cook yourself, for a few or a few hundred, the hows are here. If you hunt food in cafés instead of grocery stores, the same information can encourage and aid your personal "discoveries" of regional cuisine. Likewise, there are libraries filled with illustrated anthologies of antiques featuring invaluable historical background, definitions of terms, facts on periods, styles, craftsmanship and full-color visual aids. We encourage every serious hunter to have and study one of these. We will concentrate instead on field trials...where to go...what to look for...and how to buy.

Since getting a feel for the chronology of antiques is important to the collector and often difficult to develop, we have planned period parties...featuring in each of our three chosen countries the earliest meal of the day on the furniture of the earliest period of interest...i.e., breakfast on a 17th century table. As our "sets", which feature three centuries of decorative arts in three countries, are taken entirely from our shop inventory and/or our own collections, we have had to mix styles and periods occasionally...much as most of us would have to, or choose to, in our own homes.

Please keep in mind that while we may speak with the conviction of converts, we are not, nor do we consider ourselves to be, the world's foremost authorities on any aspect of either food or antiques. We are, however, among the world's most enthusiastic treasure hunters, we have accumulated some useful information, we have had some great adventures...and it is the pleasure of all of this that we want to share with you.

Our answers to some basic questions about antiques

Q.

What constitutes an antique?

A.

A widely accepted contemporary definition states that an antique is "a useful or decorative object, made by hand, at least 100 years old (150 for furniture) having qualities of craftsmanship, beauty, rarity or curiosity which have caused it to become valued and marketable" — a **treasure**, if you will.

The key requirements are:

     1. Handcraftsmanship

     2. Age

     3. Value

It is the first two of these requirements that distinguish authentic antiques from the popular *collectibles*, which may have value, but are largely mass produced in relatively recent times.

U.S. Customs Regulations allow duty-free import of "antiques" that are at least 100 years old. While this "100 year" standard has become the legally accepted definition of an antique, it encompasses post-Industrial-Revolution-machine-made furniture and other decorative arts that are not generally recognized as antiques by dealers and collectors.

Q.

Why buy antiques?

A.

Because antiques are one-of-a-kind objects, made by an artist or craftsperson for a particular person and/or purpose which inevitably display characteristics of the time, place and culture in which they were made while telling their own fascinating story to the person who will listen…

Because the use of even one antique piece can give charm, character, interest and historic significance to the design of a home, garden, office, restaurant, club or public building that cannot be achieved as effectively any other way…

Because, unlike mass-produced furniture and decorations which generally lose at least half their value in the time it takes to deliver them from store to home or office, antiques tend to become more valuable as they are used and enjoyed. While the potential for profit exists, of

Watch For These!

A list of antiques that are still readily available and often, we think, good value: (Some were overvalued 8-10 years ago. Prices leveled and now seem under market.)

- *19th C. Brass or Wood Candlesticks*
- *19th C. Pewter — all shapes and sizes*
- *19th C. Copper Molds and Cookware*
- *19th C. Boxes (Rapid price rise — move fast.)*
- *18th and 19th C. Brass or Copper Jardinaires and Coal Buckets*
- *16th, 17th and 19th C. Carved Wood Figures and Frames*

Watch OUT! For These

*A list of "Bewares" that might be found any place antique furniture is sold. While such pieces often have merit and may be far more desirable than a new piece, you need to be aware that they are far less valuable than "right" period antiques and they may not be labeled properly. (Your trained eye **should** spot them.)*

Reproductions *— made from old timbers or new wood that has been artificially distressed and stained.*

course, depending on what, where and how well one buys, the dedicated treasure hunters are buying to keep (not to sell), taking the profit in their pleasure and passing it on to future generations.

How does one become a successful antique hunter?

With **knowledge**. You must arm yourself with all the known facts concerning your targets or your particular interests. Since antiques can be found almost anywhere, the challenge to the hunter is to identify correctly and evaluate the find. With a lot of luck, you may acquire a great piece for a pittance. With some knowledge and a little luck, you can do the same thing with more regularity. With knowledge alone, you can always insure that what you pay for is what you get — the most practical approach to buying anything.

It's important to recognize that some hunters have an instinct for antiques: a sixth sense, if you will, for age and quality which cannot be accounted for by reason of previous knowledge or experience and which enhances the discovery/identity process immeasurably. Still, valuing for purchase requires current facts.

What are the most important factors to consider in buying an antique?

Age, Quality and **Condition**. These factors are the traditional considerations in judging an antique.

The **Age** question is just that — when was the piece made? This critical calculation is based on elements of craftsmanship, materials, style, probable origin and use.

Quality refers to more subjective questions of design, artistry, use of materials, balance and proportion.

Reconstructions — combining parts of one or more antiques with a large percentage of new wood and work. Basically a repro with some seniority.

Radical Restorations — of over-the-hill period pieces requiring so much replacement and refitting that they become quasi-antiques.

Marriages — of two antiques (or parts thereof) to make one piece which is, presumably, greater than the sum of its parts in beauty, usefulness and price. For example, an abandoned glazed top is added to a plain bureau to create a bureau bookcase, two plain chests are creatively stacked to become a chest-on-chest or an orphan rack is added to a nondescript dresser base and sold as a period Welsh Dresser.

Antiques With Major Restoration — to feet and legs, backs of chairs, tops of tables and chests, cornices, etc.

Antiques With Major "Improvements" — to make pieces more useful or beautiful (and costly) including later carving on plain early tables, a total "veneer job" on an old pine chest to give a Georgian Mahogany mien or paneled doors added to a bookcase.

Condition is the relationship between the piece as originally crafted and decorated and its current state. Has the original style, construction and finish been preserved? If repaired or altered — in what ways, to what extent and how well?

Q. How does one make valid judgments concerning these criteria?

A.

With Your Eyes and Your Fingers. A good antiquer develops an "eye" for antiques, just as a good cook develops an "eye" for produce and meat. One must look critically at each piece, separating the important details from the overall look, and use the fingers to discover things that the eye may not see — the knife marks on the inner curve of a Georgian cabriole leg or the adze marks on the plank back of a Louis XV armoire.

Q. How does a novice get the essential practical experience?

A.

A tough answer. Even people fortunate enough to have grown up with antiques often show little interest in the hunt for them until they are far from home. Museums and a few private collections have the pieces that set the standards, but seldom do they offer a hands-on learning experience. Dealers' stock could be the best training ground, but finding a dealer with the time to teach or the inclination to allow an upside down examination of his/her stock may be difficult.

Antique shows are a good place to begin. There, dealers have the same "shop" goals, to show their best wares to advantage and to convince the public to buy them, without any of the shopkeepers' nonselling responsibilities that consume their time in the shop. A few serious questions will probably entitle you to examine closely the clues to excellence — the thick cut of the early veneer, the original blocks behind the ogee bracket feet, the oak drawer lining, the period brass hardware, etc.

The same result will follow if you purchase your first antiques from a dealer who guarantees what he/she sells and makes a point of detailing age, quality and condition to the buyer. Not only will you have your own pieces for study, you will also have the dealer as a reliable source of information, since dealers generally regard the knowledgeable and/or sincerely interested buyer as their best customer. If what you learn from the dealer enables you to pick up a piece of superb Colonial craftsmanship on your next world tour, there is no offense — only a compliment to that dealer's skill as a teacher. The confidence remains that the next piece you treasure will surely be in his or her next shipment.

Q. **Are there some simple guidelines to follow?**

A. Yes. The best ones are these obvious ones:

If a piece is handmade, it will have irregularities. Check, for example, the dovetailing — the interlocking construction of furniture tops, drawer linings, and metal containers — a technique of early craftsmanship that is still employed in machine production. The early hand-cut dovetails (even those formed by the most meticulous craftsman) are irregular in one or more measurements while the modern machine-cut variety are perfectly proportioned on every part of the piece. Hand-tied rugs and hand-woven tapestries display similar irregularities on the back side where the seasoned collector looks first. Early furniture that has been sanded and polished to perfection on the "meant-to-show" surfaces will reveal adze marks to the fingertips and natural discoloration to the eye on the backs and undersides of the same piece.

If a piece was completed 100 years ago or more it should look old, even to the untrained eye and even if it has been restored, refinished or polished, whether it is a wing chair, a chest of drawers, a porcelain bowl, a carpet or a candlestick. On such a piece, there should be indications of use and wear in logical places and/or changes in color and appearance due to atmospheric conditions. The earlier the piece is supposed to be, the more evidence of damage, deterioration and/or restoration one should expect to find. While patches, splices and replaced parts are not particularly desireable, they are definite signs of age. (Worm holes were a reliable indication of age until fakers began using old wormy wood in new construction.)

Construction methods offer many clues. For example, early furniture was "joined" by the mortise and tenon method. Unless the piece was painted, an examination of joints will reveal the ends of the wooden pegs that hold the piece together. Planing was done by hand with relatively primitive tools that left irregular marks, even on finished surfaces. Unfortunately, since fakers and reproduction artists have found it worth their time to use early methods and tools, construction methods are no longer, by themselves, sufficient clues to age.

Q. What about period and style?

A. The decorative arts have undergone numerous style changes over the centuries. The earliest civilizations in Egypt, Greece and Rome had their own styles which have returned repeatedly as "revivals" of fashion. The decorative void of the Dark and Middle Ages was filled magnifi-

TREASURES CHART DATES	ENGLISH MONARCH	ENGLISH PERIOD*	AMERICAN PERIOD*	FRENCH PERIOD*	CHART GENERAL STYLE*
1558-1603	Elizabeth I	Elizabethan		Renaissance (1515-1610)	Gothic (1160-1620)
1603-1625	James I	Jacobean		Louis XIII (1610-1643)	Baroque (1620-1700)
1625-1649	Charles I	Carolean	Colonial (1625-1700)	Louis XIV (1643-1715)	
1649-1660	Commonwealth	Cromwellian			
1660-1685	Charles II	Restoration (or Charles II)			
1685-1689	James II				
1689-1694	William & Mary	William & Mary			
1694-1702	William III	William III			Rococo (1695-1760)
1702-1714	Anne	Queen Anne	William & Mary (1700-1725)		
1714-1727	George I	Early Georgian		Régence (1715-1723)	
1727-1760	George II		Queen Anne (1725-1755)	Louis XV (1723-1774)	
1760-1811	George III	Late Georgian	Chippendale (1755-1790)		Neoclassical (1755-1805)
			Federal (1785-1815)	Louis XVI (1774-1793)	
				Directoire (1793-1799)	
				Empire (1799-1815)	Empire (1799-1815)
1812-1820	George III	Regency	American Empire (1815-1840)	Restauration (1815-1830)	Regency (1812-1830)
1820-1830	George IV				
1830-1837	William IV	William IV		Louis Philippe (1830-1848)	Eclectic (1830-1880)
1837-1901	Victoria	Victorian	Victorian (1840-1900)		
				2nd Empire (1848-1870)	
				3rd Republic (1871-1940)	Arts & Crafts (1880-1900)
1901-1910	Edward VII	Edwardian	Art Nouveau (1900-1920)		Art Nouveau (1900-1920)

Period and style dates are approximate.

*Country craftsmen generally
copied the furniture styles
which they or their customers
saw in the cities, perhaps
years after the style was
introduced or years after the
style's popularity had waned.
Therefore, we can consider
provincial furniture as
"period" even though it
may have been made as much
as 20 — sometimes 30 — years
after the designated dates.*

cently by the Renaissance in Western Europe with styles moving from the sumptuously ornate baroque to the sensuously swirling rococo. Fashion became foremost in late 17th and early 18th century Europe — and in Europe's colonies. Changes in style have reflected changes in the political, religious, and economic climate. As royalty superseded the church as the dominant patron of the arts, emphasis and subject matter were permanently shifted. The differing living conditions in different countries resulted in different styles which, in turn, influenced the styles of their neighbors and trading partners.

Knowledgeable collectors should be able to identify the major English, French and American styles indicated in the chart on the previous page. The best way to become familiar with style differences and similarities is to buy and study one of the dozens of lavishly illustrated, well documented books on the subject (often available at "publisher's close-out" prices). It's important to remember, however, that the **style does not establish the age** of any decorative art. All it does tell about the age of any given piece is that it cannot be any earlier than the style it represents. A chair crafted after a design in Thomas Chippendale's *The Gentleman and Cabinet-Maker Director* may have been made in London in 1760 or in Grand Rapids in 1930 — or in North Carolina yesterday. If the piece was crafted during the initial development of a particular style it is referred to as **Period**. If crafted during a revival of interest in an earlier style, it is a **Reproduction**. Repros may be quite valuable, depending on how early and how well they were made, **but it is the period piece of good quality in good condition that is coveted by museums and collectors throughout the world and, thus, commands the top price.**

Please note that indiscriminate reliance on style as

an indication of age is a trap that catches both amateur and professional. Too many dealers, auctioneers and appraisers base their value judgments of supposed antiques on style without regard to the other evidence. Too many "antique price guides" list only the style of a piece and not the date, rendering the stated value useless. Style is only one clue, not the entire answer.

Q. **How much is any antique worth?**

A. Hands up on this one. Since every antique is unique the "simple" answer is that it's worth what someone is willing to pay for it. A good friend once asked advice on the price of a Chippendale mirror that was quite expensive and had to be shipped from the East Coast. The only reasonable response was: "If it's guaranteed to be as described; if it's what you really want; if this is their best price and you are willing to pay it plus the shipping costs — then the mirror must be worth that much."

However, on a treasure hunt, the system is "know your market." It is up to the buyer to shop around enough to be familiar with retail prices within his or her particular area of interest. For instance, if you know from observing several examples in shops — or auction catalogues (an excellent collector's resource) — that well-designed English Broad-arm Windsor Chairs, c. 1860, in good original condition sell for $1,300 to $1,800, then you can grin and grab the "flea market $800 special" that you judge to be similar in all respects. Getting the range of prices is not an easy process, but it is possible if you are willing to take the time to price-shop the antique stores, flea markets and estate sales in your area, study the "dated" price guides and keep current on auction results...particularly in New York. If study fails, there is nothing like a money mistake

English Windsor Chair (narrow arm) with crinoline stretcher, c. 1860, popular seating in 19th C. Pubs.

"Collectibles" are not antiques. They are either old, mass-produced things that have become more popular and, thus, more valuable over the years or they are things that are newly mass produced in "limited editions". Since collectibles are seldom inexpensive, it's difficult for some of us to understand why anyone would choose to "hunt" them instead of real antiques, but any hunt is better than none.

— spending when you should not or not spending when you should — to make you a better hunter next time.

Provenance (the documented history of a piece) and/or **Source** (the estate or collection from which it comes to market) can make an enormous difference in the public's view of antique value, particularly in today's volatile market.

Provenance, in the sense of being able to prove who made a piece or exactly when and for whom it was made, has always been a factor in the price of antiques, particularly the finer pieces. A signed piece is considered more valuable than an unsigned one. A bed that can be proven by written documents to have comforted George Washington overnight is thought to be worth significantly more than one where he "might" have slept. Not only do signatures and records prove a date, they add to the prestige and romance of a piece— and, thus, logically to the price, particularly if the creator or original owner was important.

Today, "possible" provenance has become a marketing tool of a few highly imaginative, if not unscrupulous, dealers. Unless a maker's mark/signature or family documents are available, the three paragraph "history" that one often finds on antique price tags must be considered rumor or conjecture and should not, in our opinion, add to the price (although believing what is written may add to your pleasure of ownership).

Source, in the sense of being able to prove, for example, that a piece is from a particular castle, is really part of the provenance. Today, source has another meaning, largely promoted by the auction houses: what person or what museum or what corporation thought enough of this piece to add it to the collection? If this owner is important enough, just temporary possession can add to the estimate

17th C. Welsh Dresser

or public perception of value. Focus on source has been so effective economically in the sale rooms that obscure collectors are frequently cited along with major ones in the hope that previous ownership by any old collector will add to the bidder's interest. Whether or not source adds to value, it often adds to price.

There is no "list price" for antiques. There is a reasonable price range, that can be determined by a study of the current market, for all but the rarest pieces. Determining what you can and should pay for a particular piece may be easier with these basic rules: never spend more than you can comfortably afford, no matter how much you like a piece. Never buy a piece you don't like, no matter how cheap it is. Always buy the best piece you can afford, making sure that the price is in line with that of similar pieces.

Q. How do you know you're getting the 'real thing'?

A. The most important question of all and the hardest to answer. As much as they know and as hard as they try, the "world's foremost authorities" get fooled from time to time. Today's collector must recognize that, historically, as soon as the treasures of a civilization – artifacts, stone carvings, metals, paintings, bronzes, Chippendale chairs and other precious items – have become popular enough to be valuable, they have become valuable enough to be copied. The more valuable, the more expert the copies. So far, nobody is faking late Victorian and Edwardian furniture because the possible return is not worth the labor, but that's not true of Queen Anne or William and Mary pieces.

When the price of a genuine Queen Anne Welsh Dresser reaches 12,000 pounds Sterling ($22,000) then a skilled craftsman will try to copy it perfectly. He may sell

---

Where Are
The Bargains?

*They are out there somewhere,
waiting for you. These are
likely places:*

Garage/Tag/Yard Sales *—
Whatever your region calls
these "let's get rid of this old
stuff" sales, they are hot
prospects for hunters with
more time than money. The
best bet is the sale with an ad
that mentions "antiques"
without a specific listing. The
owner knows he/she has something, but may not know what
it is or how much it is worth.*

Estate Sales *— The best, most
consistent, prospect because
such sales tend to include a
wide variety of items of all
ages that must, for legal
reasons, be sold in a short time
— often to a low, "left" bid.*

Auctions: City and Country *—
The record high prices happen
here, as do the low ones. Big
cities offer so many sales that
your chances for "sleepers"
may be better there than at
the once-a-year sale that
attracts everyone in smaller
communities.*

Flea Markets *— Permanent
ones (everyday or every
weekend) are poor prospects
compared to the once-a-year
(or month) variety. Go **very**
early to these — before the
scheduled opening.
(continued)*

it for just the copy it is, but the next owner may not. When a single 18th century American chair sells for almost three million dollars, the incentive to sell a repro as a "period" original becomes almost irresistible.

What we're saying is that, given what we all know about the popularity and price of most genuine antiques today, the intelligent buyer must assume that the "Louis XV commode" at the "surprisingly modest price" was probably made yesterday and is one more example of the truth of the saying that, "if something seems too good to be true, it probably is!"

But it is not just the recently made reproduction that one needs to recognize. Most earlier periods have had popular revivals so that today there are many 100 year old reproductions on the market — 19th century pieces that are copied after those of an earlier era and which are difficult to distinguish from the period pieces of that earlier time. These repros, often handsomely made, are generally valuable in their own right, but the dedicated hunter still needs to distinguish them from the earlier period pieces to get proper value per dollar.

Of course, if you buy from a reputable dealer who knows and guarantees his/her stock, then you have what the piece is represented to be or you can return it. If you buy "at risk" then you must abide by the old legal term *caveat emptor* and assume the risk of acquiring a fake. Regardless of where and how you buy, you will want to determine the amount of restoration that has occurred and take that into consideration in deciding whether the piece and the price are for you.

Experience indicates that developing the ability to see a piece for what it is is possible for most serious collectors willing to study and then get the requisite experience. (As in every field, there are a few exceptions who find that

Antique Shops — New shops often have pieces that new owners don't yet recognize or value properly. Eclectic shops may have pieces that are underpriced because of dealer's error, dis-interest or customer policy of passing on the good buys. You can cash in on all of these probabilities, but you must make the rounds often.

Speaking of shops, don't forget that today's reasonable retail price may seem like a rare bargain in two years — and is sure to seem like one in ten.

their talents lean in other directions.) As we venture through the English, French, and American chapters, we will point out specific traps and dangers — pitfalls which will challenge your knowledge and ability and, in the process, add to the excitement of the hunt.

Q.

And finally — what and where are the best places to buy antiques?

A.

Anywhere in the world...if you know what you are doing...and you surely will after reading this book. To prove the point, we have purchased antiques for Sebree Galleries over the last five years in Hungary, Romania, Yugoslavia, East/West and North Africa, Israel, Turkey, India, Nepal, Indonesia, Malaysia, Singapore, Hong Kong, China, Japan, Argentina, Chile, Peru, Mexico and, of course, Western Europe and the United States.

Our list of specific sources? Within the text of this book we have listed **every region and city where we shop for the major part of our inventory** including details of the best markets. These specific places we mention in England, France and the U.S. are traditional sources of antiques for dealers. While the standards of quality and quantity of antiques change frequently and sometimes radically within the individual shops, sending us to the guidebooks for new possibilities, they have not changed significantly within the regions during our long hunting experience.

It's clear that the hunt for antiques is going on today everywhere, all of the time, and can provide a challenging reason to be anywhere, any time. But if travel is not your style, not to worry, the best place to find antiques today may be right where you are!

ENGLISH

A Breakfast at Bermondsey

The Hunt Country Brunch

Pub Lunch at Portobello

Tea in the Georgian City

A Regency Theatre Supper

A Breakfast at Bermondsey

BILL of FARE

**Breakfast
at Bermondsey**

Market Cheddar Pie

Squire's Bacon

Gooseberry Chutney

Grilled Stuffed Tomato

Welsh Treacle Torte

Steaming Hot White Coffee

Public Markets are an ancient tradition in England. Towns and cities developed around them and they remain important centers of social activity today. Part of the immense fascination of London for antiquers is that it is actually made up of a lot of villages and their markets.

One of these is New Caledonian Market, better known as Bermondsey. The single most exciting moment in 22 years of the antique business was our first Bermondsey visit. It was 1971 and we were in England on our maiden European buying trip, thrilled to be stocking from the source rather than from other dealers and terrified by the certain uncertainties of what, where and how to accomplish the task.

This idealized market stall is a collection of our favorite things. We list them by subject for continuity.

TEXTILES
1, 17, 37: 17th C. Tapestry Fragments. (37 is applied to pillow); 2, 29: 19th C. Armorial Needlework; 5: 19th C. (early) Drapery Tie/Tassels (one of pair); 20: 19th C. Hunt Trophy Hide; 24, 26: 18th C. Silk Clerical Accessories (Early textiles are racing ahead in prices with many dealers specializing now. Provincial markets and U.S. house sales are best sources.)

CARVINGS
4, 8, 9, 10, 11, 33, 34: 16th/17th C. Wood Carvings and Panels; 28: 18th C. Carved Wood Figure (Santo); 31, 38: 18th/15th C. Stone Carvings (Such carvings are the best buys in the markets and in many shops. Even the expensive ones may be undervalued.)

COATS OF ARMS
3: 19th C. Painted Cast Iron, Royal Arms of England; 19: 18th C. Oil on Wood Panel; 21: 18th C. Brass Repoussé Plaque; 32: 18th C. Oil on Canvas; — 2, 10, and 29 repeat in this category. (Coats of Arms appear on all kinds of objects, in various forms from all periods. Even the late ones, if handmade, are worth collecting.)

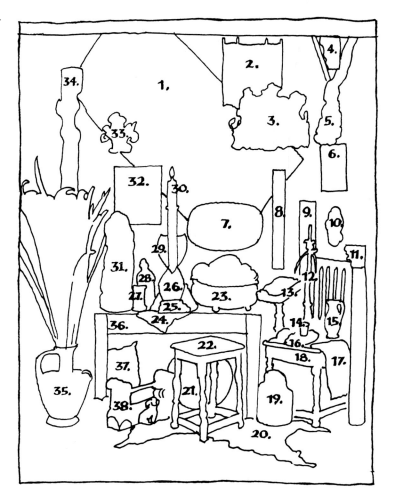

An ad in one of the collector's magazines had led us to a shipper who would collect our English purchases, pack them into a sea container and arrange transport to our choice of U.S. ports. The ad suggested hiring a courier to drive us around the countryside taking us to the appropriate dealers and handling all paper work. It was a good idea for beginners, which we fortunately accepted — otherwise it might have been years before we knew about the London markets.

Bermondsey is a south London outdoor "dealers" market which is held every Friday morning of the year (Christmas Day excepted) in mist, rain, snow, sun or in-between. Legally, it is not supposed to open until daylight, in accordance with an ancient English common law which still prevails insisting that a buyer must be able to see the merchandise. (Actually, long before the sun comes up, the serious buyers use their *torches* to search for the best antiques pieces before the competition arrives. We have tried this with as much success as if we had been buying with blindfolds.)

More than 500 dealers from all over England have individual stalls set up on several blocks at the intersection of Bermondsey Road and Long Lane. The neighborhood is warehouse/low-income housing where it is perfectly safe to park and walk (as long as the place you park has an unexpired meter). Easier yet is to take a cab from your hotel. There are plenty of cabbies about before dawn in London, and they just assume that any Americans hailing them that early on Friday are going to Bermondsey. It's an easy 20-minute, 5 to 6 pound ($9-$11) ride from the West End and, as long as you find a cab before the market begins to close down (about 11:30 a.m.), you can easily return to your hotel the same way.

Forget breakfast at the hotel — it's too early. Plan to have coffee from a street stall when you first arrive, shop one of the blocks, then have breakfast at Bermondsey. Dress comfortably and warmly (it will seem much colder at the market than it does just outside your hotel) and be prepared to continue buying even in the rain. The stall holders put up plastic sheets and ignore both drip and downpour. Bring at least one large shopping bag to hold your umbrella, scarf, extra socks and treasure horde.

What awaits the treasure hunter at Bermondsey? Although the stall size and the risk of bad weather limit the number of large furniture pieces, there are some available, particularly around the perimeter of each block. We frequently find Georgian tables in need of minimal repair and 19th century Windsor chairs (watch for and ask about res-

EARLY METALWARES
BRASS: 23: 17th C. Footed Repoussé Bowl; 35: 18th C. Milk Jug; 21: 18th C. Brass Repoussé Plaque; COPPER: 13: 19th C. Roasting Pan; PEWTER: 7: 18th C. French Repoussé Platter; 14, 15, 16, 27: 19th C. English Ale Mugs, Plate and Claret Jug (We think it is a good time to buy these early metals.)

CANDLESTICKS
12: 19th C. Brass Altar Stick; 35: 18th C. Polychromed Wood Stick (There are some repros around, particularly in the miniatures, but the 19th C. brass, bronze and wood pieces, and 18th C. wood are still plentiful and often under-valued.)

SMALLS
6: Early Mirrors and 25: Leather-bound Books are frequently found in markets at reasonable prices.

EARLY OAK
18, 22, 36: 17th C. English Chair, Joynt Stool and Console Table (Furniture of this period is now hard to find and expensive, although we still find bits and bargains in the markets. Better buys are the early oak wood carvings, boxes and architectural pieces.)

English Oak Wainscot Chair
c. 1650

toration) and have found Welsh dressers, joint stools, cricket tables and other early pine tables — all 19th century. We always find great boxes — 17th century Bible holders or 18th century writing boxes and late Victorian glove, handkerchief, and military cases.

There is no better place in England for *smalls* — the myriad treasures which can be carried home in a suitcase — estate jewelry, Georgian and Victorian silver, brass and wood-twist candlesticks, copper jelly molds, bronze boxes and figures, early wood carvings (which are probably the best 16th-18th century antiques still available in quantity and at relatively reasonable prices), English and Oriental ceramics, magnifying glasses, brass fire tools, unique weather houses and much, much more.

Age of items ranges from early Egyptian to late yesterday and origin is "the world." Of particular interest are the English traditionals — not necessarily very old, but very English and very decorative — such items as military drums, uniforms and buttons, nautical paraphenalia and ship models, horsey/hunt regalia and late Victoriana including stuffed animals under glass. In the one building that is actually part of the market (a hulky buff and brown two-story on the corner of Bermondsey Road and Long Lane) there is an entire section devoted to jewelry and another to antique leather bound books. A corner of the second floor shelters the best of the food stalls where you should have breakfast. It's a 'some sit, most stand, no-atmosphere-but-the-people' situation with great bangers, homemade cheese, treacle or gooseberry pie, egg and English bacon sandwiches and "white" coffee, and one can expect the same excellent food quality served by the same cooks, year after year. Our pleasure in this oft-repeated experience cannot be overstated — especially when we're there on a misty, chilly, proper English day.

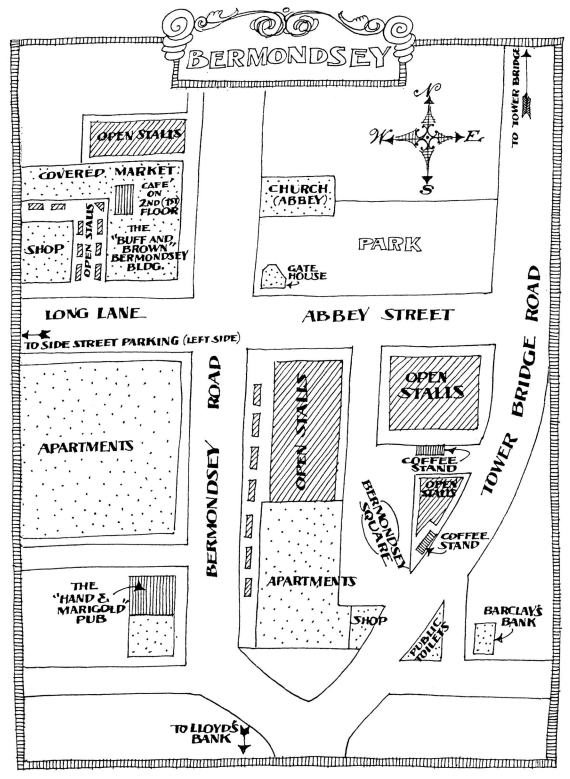

TREASURES

Bermondsey Market — London (South)
Every Friday. Daylight to 11:30 a.m. (approximately)
Across Tower Bridge to Long Lane at Bermondsey Road

Like the treasures, the treasure hunters at Bermondsey are from everywhere...Hasidic Jews stroking their long beards in contemplation of a fine example of Georgian silver; Germans and French who are determined to bargain in their own languages; ladies from Dallas, swathed in Burberrys and calling to each other across the stalls in unmistakable drawls; fashionably attired English dealers who come early, buy unobtrusively and depart in time to open their Mayfair shops by 10 a.m. At ten o'clock, some of the sellers are packing up too and, by noon, the antique dealers are gone, leaving only a smattering of stalls with "tourist" goods for the late-rising shoppers.

As fascinating as the buyers are the sellers. Most of them are English — from the counties just north, south and east of London — who search all week for the stall full of treasures to display each Friday and who must turn these goods for at least a small profit in order to return with different pieces the following week. Their concern about dress is only to be warm, dry or cool enough, but there is an admirable style about their look and manner — and the superb Oxford English that most speak. Actually, the conversation is a problem with English dealers at market. They are so pleased to see their friends and stall neighbors and have so much news to exchange that it is frequently necessary to interrupt these proceedings if you want to buy.

How does the amateur buy in a dealer's market? Obvious tourists might encounter some indifference here but pretending to be a dealer is not recommended. Be forthright, businesslike and polite, just as you would be back home. Most dealers have come, after all, to sell to the first person who wants the piece and has the money. The tradition of English antique markets is not that of the souk/bazaar where the seller begins with an absurdly high price and the buyer responds with an equally ridiculous low

offer. In English Markets, the price is generally clearly marked and most English dealers, whether because of competition or other market conditions, do not put a large percentage of profit on their goods. It is always fair to ask, "Is that the best price?" Sometimes it is and then you must decide how much you want the piece. If a lower price is offered, that will be the last price on the piece unless other pieces interest you and you become a volume buyer.

The best psychology, we find, in buying a quantity of antiques anywhere is to establish the best price on the first piece that really interests you and, if it's reasonable, say, "I'll take it", thus getting the dealer's serious attention. The move from "looker" to "customer" is through the barrier to any special pricing or other privileges. Markets are all cash and carry, so do take along plenty of pounds Sterling. U.S. bills and traveler's checks are difficult to convert on the spot and diminish buying power, even when the dealer agrees to take them. There are two banks near Bermondsey that open at 9:30 a.m. where you can exchange money if you do run short (Barclays is closer, across from the toilets; Lloyd's is on down Tower Bridge Road). Another important neighborhood center is the pub across Bermondsey Road — The Hand and Marigold — which also features decent lager, cider and toilet facilities (loos). You may find it worth the price of a half-pint to take advantage of this pub stop which, with its early morning regulars, joins Bermondsey Market as treasures to be hunted and savored by Anglophiles from everywhere.

Market Cheddar Pie

Nothing is more welcome to a cold and weary market shopper than this creamy cheese pie. The taste can be varied by the addition of country ham, peppers, or grilled vegetables.

1 loaf Brioche or firm white bread, sliced 1/4" thick, crusts trimmed
16 oz. grated English Sharp Cheddar Cheese
8 oz. Gruyere Cheese, grated
2 T. butter
1/4 lb. Shitake mushrooms
1 leek, finely minced
6 eggs beaten
2 C. Half and Half
2 C. crème fraiche mixed with 2 cloves roasted garlic, minced
salt & pepper
1 tsp. Colman's Dry Mustard
pinch freshly grated nutmeg

Sauté leek and mushrooms in butter until soft. Layer bread, cheese, leek and mushrooms in buttered glass baking dish 7" x 11" (2 layers each). Mix together eggs, Half & Half, crème fraiche, and spices. Pour liquid over bread and cheese layers. Let it sit about 30 minutes. Bake at 375 degrees for 30 minutes or until center is firm.

Squire's Bacon

Mustard seeds have been cultivated by the English since Roman times. The combination of a truly fine country bacon with an English marmalade and mustard coating make this bacon irresistible. It is especially good as a filling for scones or just on a toothpick as an appetizer.

1 lb. Wiltshire Bacon (or any thickly sliced smoked bacon)
3/4 C. Orange Marmalade
2 T. Colman's Hot Mustard
Brown Sugar
Orange Zest

Layer bacon on a cookie sheet lined with parchment paper. Brush bacon with mixture of marmalade and mustard. (You may also use an herbed jelly such as rosemary.) Sprinkle lightly with brown sugar and zest. Bake at 450 degrees until brown.

Welsh Treacle Torte

Treacle Torte originated in the Midlands as an inexpensive dessert for factory workers. The addition of lemon juice and zest make this version less sweet, but rather more satisfying. These may also be prepared as "mini" tarts for tea.

Short Crust — Pâté "Brisée":
1 C. flour
1 T. sugar
1/2 stick butter
1/4 tsp. lemon peel
1 T. water
1 tsp. vanilla

Cut butter into dry ingredients until it has a cornmeal texture. Mix lemon peel, water and vanilla together and sprinkle over this mixture. Knead lightly and roll out dough on lightly floured board. Line individual tart pans and let them rest in refrigerator for 30 minutes.

Filling (mix together):
3 eggs
1/4 C. bread crumbs
zest and juice of 1 small lemon
1 C. Golden Syrup
1/2 C. cream

Fill pastry with this mixture and bake at 375 degrees for 20 minutes or until custard is set.

Gooseberry Chutney

Tart gooseberries are the perfect chutney fruit as they have a wonderful tangy flavor. Try using this on a scone or biscuit and ham sandwich.

1 lb. gooseberries
1/2 C. sugar
8 T. malt vinegar
1 clove garlic, minced
1 tsp. chopped fresh ginger
1/2 tsp. salt
pinch of cinnamon, cloves,
    allspice, and white pepper
1/4 C. raisins
1/2 C. red onion, chopped finely
1 T. jalapeno pepper, minced
1 tsp. Dijon mustard

Combine sugar and vinegars. Bring to a boil over low heat. Stir until the sugar dissolves then add ginger, garlic, and spices. Stir to combine. Add gooseberries and raisins and simmer until fruit is tender (approximately 20 minutes). Strain fruit and return juice to pan. Simmer this mixture until it is "syrupy." Add onion, peppers and mustard. Simmer 5 minutes and add gooseberries and raisins. Let cool. Can be prepared 2 days ahead.

The Hunt Country Brunch

BILL of FARE

Hunt Country Brunch

————

Cotswold Lamb
with Red Currant Sauce

Manor Garden Asparagus
and Root Vegetables

Wye Valley Salmon
with Sorrel

Cock-a-Leekies

Country Cheddar with
Fresh Fruit

————

Hot Mulled Wine or Ale

The travel guide photo of the Lygon Arms in Broadway features red-coated huntsmen gathered with horses and hounds in front of this stunning 16th century Cotswold stone coaching inn. To us, as to many other travelers, the picture-perfect Cotswold villages are the essence of English Country, and it is there that we like to headquarter on our frequent buying trips. Frankly, during a dozen or so stopovers at the Lygon, we have never found a huntsman in the front drive, and we have never found the Cotswolds a good place for dealers to buy. It's the original gnarled oak beams and posts in the bedrooms, the roaring Inglenook fires in the public rooms and the classic four-course English dinners (with "grouse pie in season") at

The wooly texture and warm colors of tapestries and Oriental rugs are the perfect background for early oak furniture in a Cotswold manor house. Pewter, copper, pottery and wood were the 17th century's accessories. (We have a few anachronisms in every antique composite — deliberately — to indicate the enormous choice of treasures that might fit into such a scene today.) 1. English Oak Dresser Base with Paneled Doors and Marquetry Drawer Trim, c. 1720; 2. Flemish Tapestry, c. 1830; 3. Turkish Runner, c. 1935; 4. English Copper Fish Poacher, c. 1860; 5. Wedgwood Game Dish, c. 1870; 6. English Pewter Shepherd's Lunch Pail, c. 1840; 7. North African Carved Wood Stand, c. 1880; 8. Dutch Turned Wood Casket Candlestick with Polychrome (multi-color paint) Finish; 9. English Porcelain Decanter with Armorial Decoration, c. 1900; 10. Pewter Tankard, c. 1790; 11. English Oval Copper Container with Repoussé Armorial Shield.

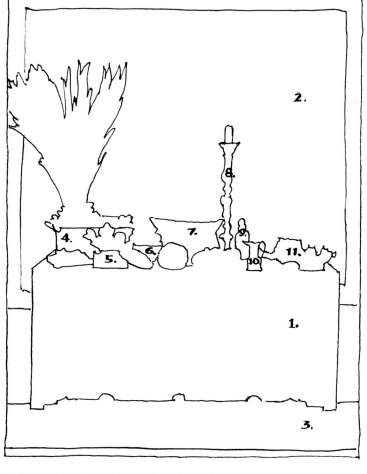

this ancient hostelry, plus the misty morning walks between shops in nearby Chipping Campden, Moreton-in-March, Stow-on-the-Wold and Burford that lure us back year after year.

Each of these historic market towns has several antique shops (between the pubs) and they are close enough together to be discovered in a day or so. Even though Bourton-on-the-Water (don't miss the miniature village or the bird sanctuary), Upper and Lower Slaughter and Bibury are not antique stops, they are still worth a special visit in order to experience in full measure the story-book charm that is the indisputable treasure of this part of the world. Also, while in the Cotswolds, use the *AA Large-scale Map* of the countryside to find your way

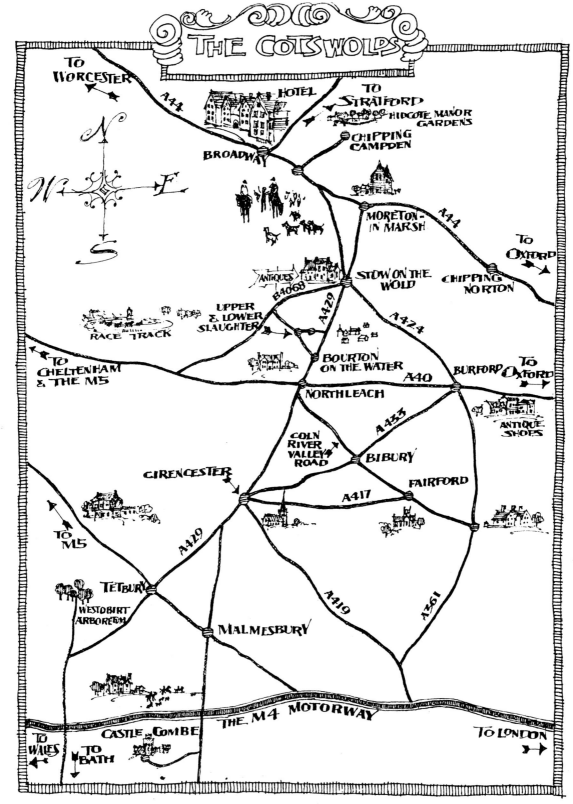

TREASURES

The Cotswolds — 1-1/2 - 2 Hours West of London

down the Coln River valley, past 10th century churches and 14th century manor houses, before taking the main roads to the clusters of antique shops in Fairford, Lechlade, Cirencester, Malmesbury, and Tetbury.

There is a manor house-cum-hotel in or near each Cotswold village, at prices ranging from reasonable to very expensive, where to spend a night is to retreat to another century. Less dramatic, but equally pleasant and far easier on the pounds/dollars, are the traditional pub/hotels and B & Bs located throughout the Cotswolds — each offering its unique version of the "Old English" experience.

In our view, the Cotswold antique shops, particularly those in Stow-on-the-Wold (plan on three to four hours to see all the shops there) offer the retail buyer England's largest, easily accessible selection of early English furniture. While the prices match or exceed those of similar goods in London, the quantity of very early (back to Gothic) pieces is astonishing and a must for anyone looking for superb early oak or walnut. But don't despair if you are not after "period and expensive" — most villages have an antique center with many individual stalls offering goods similar to the street markets. The best way to decide where to go for antiques in the Cotswolds, or anywhere else in England for that matter, is to buy a copy of *Guide to the Antique Shops of Britain* published by Antique Collectors' Club, Ltd. and available at many shops and bookstores. Read through the listings for each shop in towns or cities you will visit. The information on shop size, location, hours and stock is invaluable to a treasure hunter and can save lots of precious travel time (plan to average about 30 mph on your drives between villages unless you can utilize the motorways — England's high-speed version of our Interstates).

In addition to furniture — French as well as English — the Cotswolds' shops offer an infinite selection of traditional forms in English boxes and caddies, potteries and porcelains, and copper, brass and pewter, most of which are suitable for suitcase shipping. Still good buys are 18th century repoussé brass jardinaires with armorial designs, unusual 19th century brass candlesticks and 19th century copper stock pots/sauce pans. Although some of these items will need boxing, they could be checked through on the airplane with little risk.

While we understand the compulsion to buy the perfect piece during the perfect trip, we have to tell you that buying and shipping only one or a few pieces from Europe to the United States is seldom economical. Unless the piece you choose is very expensive, you may well find that the cost of getting it home is greater than the purchase price. However, if you do find a piece of furniture that you must have, the Cotswold dealer can undoubtedly arrange shipping for you.

The hunt for regional cuisine in the Cotswolds is easily rewarded in the early oak-beamed pubs on every corner. However, the ultimate Cotswold experience is manor-house life which you should indulge in while you're here — with a hunt brunch, lunch, afternoon tea or a game dinner. You'll find such gastronomical treasures in and between every village.

You can reach the Cotswolds by train from London, and rent a car on arrival, or hire a car and driver. We prefer to drive ourselves in England so that we are free to stop every time we see an *Antiques* sign. Howsoever you choose to get there, do not miss the hunt for food and antiques in the Cotswolds. The villages, the shops, the inns, the pubs, the sights and the people — all are treasures of a lifetime!

Cotswold Lamb

Grilling meats is a highly regarded profession in England with few honored master chefs allowed to wear the respected "black cap." Using fruit tree branches or vines over coals makes a truly divine flavor for almost any meat.

1 — 3-4 lb. spring leg of lamb
3 cloves of garlic, slivered
salt & pepper

Wash lamb, pat dry, stud with garlic slivers, and salt and pepper. Place twigs from fruit trees or grape vines over medium hot coals scattered evenly over bottom of grill. Place leg of lamb on grill with lid tightly sealed. Rotate lamb every 15 minutes (3 rotations). Baste with sauce and place, covered, in low oven to keep warm.

Sauce:
8 oz. currant or cherry jelly
4 oz. butter
4 oz. chili sauce
1/2 C. finely chopped mint
  leaves (must be fresh)
salt & pepper
1/8 tsp. minced garlic
1/8 tsp. dried mustard

Heat in medium saucepan and adjust seasonings. This may be spooned over each serving of lamb. It should be made the day before so that the flavors have a chance to "marry."

Wye Valley Salmon with Sorrel Cream

Sorrel is a "lemony" herb that makes fish and vegetables taste quite fresh. Enjoy this lemon "surprise" when sorrel is added to fresh green and pasta salads. We have included two versions of this salmon. The hot one (described first) starts with a grilled salmon while the cold one is poached. Take your pick.

Hot Version:

1 — 5-7 lb. fresh salmon
6 tsp. olive oil

Hot Sorrell Cream

3 C. clam juice
5 C. dry white wine
1/4 C. dried & fresh tarragon
1 C. minced shallots
2 cloves garlic, minced
5 C. whipping cream
2 C. sour cream
2 C. sorrel, blanched, minced
    and squeezed dry
2 C. minced mushrooms,
    sautéed until dry in a small
    amount of butter
3/4 C. parsley, minced
3/4 lb. butter

Cold Version:

1 — 5-7 lb. whole salmon
2-1/2 sticks butter
1 C. shallots, minced
2 C. mushrooms, minced
1 clove garlic, minced

Cold Sorrel Cream:

1 C. tarragon vinegar
3 T. Dijon mustard
1 C. minced sorrel
2 cloves garlic
1 C. olive oil
3 C. sour cream

Brush salmon with 6 teaspoons olive oil. Grill over low coals, turning gently until firm to the touch.

Hot Sorrell Cream — in large saucepan reduce first five ingredients to 1/2 of original amount. Lower heat and add whipping cream and sour cream. Reduce sauce again until quite thick. Add sorrel, mushrooms, and parsley. Whisk in 3/4 lb. of butter, a few tablespoons at a time. After all butter is incorporated, check for seasonings and remove from heat.

To poach salmon (for cold version) — rinse salmon and pat dry. Prepare the fish poacher (or large, long pan) by filling it with 1/2 bottle white wine, 2 coarsely cut lemons, 1/2 onion, 2 carrots, celery, tarragon, salt and pepper and 3 cloves garlic (bruised). Place fish (wrapped in cheese cloth) in pan and fill with water to cover. Measure thickness of fish at widest part and simmer 10 minutes per 1". Let the fish cool in this liquid — overnight if need be. Remove fish and gently remove skin. Be careful not to tear flesh. Serve with cold sorrel cream.

Cold Sorrel Cream — combine vinegar, mustard, sorrel, and garlic in food processor and process until smooth. With the machine running, add the olive oil very slowly until it is all incorporated. It will be fairly thick. Add all of sour cream and process again until smooth. Let this cream set overnight and then taste for addition of salt and white pepper.

Cock-a-Leekies

Grilled leeks are a wonderful accompaniment for crusty meats. Their sweetness seem to enhance the meat flavors. This is also good as a light lunch served with fresh fruit.

Sauce:

1/4 C. tarragon vinegar
1/4 C. dry white wine
2 T. minced shallot
1 tsp. fresh tarragon
salt & pepper
3 egg yolks, beaten
6 oz. butter, room temperature
6 spring leeks
1/4 lb. thinly sliced
    Cumberland ham

Reduce vinegar, wine, shallot, tarragon, salt and pepper to 1/4 C. Gently whisk egg yolks into wine reduction. Continue to whisk while adding small bits of butter. Remove from heat.

Cut off all but 1" of the leek's green top and clean very carefully. Brush leek with olive oil, fresh herbs, and roasted garlic, minced. Place on medium hot coals turning every 8-10 minutes. Let cool. Wrap each leek with Cumberland salt-cured ham.

Pastry:

4-1/2 C. flour
2 tsp. salt
12 oz. unsalted butter, room
    temperature
2 eggs
2 T. milk

Place flour, salt and butter in food processor. Process until ingredients resemble coarse meal. Mix eggs and milk together and, while processor is running, add milk and egg mixture. Continue mixing until ball is formed. Refrigerate one hour. Roll pastry out into a rectangular shape on a lightly floured board. Place individual leeks in pastry rectangles and cover with 1/4 C. sauce. Seal pastry and place seam side down on lightly oiled cookie sheet. With remaining pastry, form a braid. Place on top and egg wash to seal. Refrigerate 30 minutes. Bake at 375 degrees for 20 minutes or until pastry is brown.

Creative Centerpieces

While building our catering business, we have had the most fun visiting garage and estate sales, auctions, and flea markets hunting for unique centerpieces such as unusual bowls, architectural "wonders", serving and accent pieces. Every hostess should have entertaining in mind when shopping these sales.

Visiting your local food market, whether it be city, farmer's or ethnic, will also certainly inspire the creative hostess. The sight, smells, and activities of these markets bring out the best in any cook. It is possible to find not only your dinner but your centerpiece as well.

As you can see throughout the pages of this book, we have combined foods for color, texture, and dramatic effect. Make food the star!

The following steps will assist you in creating this special look. Supplies needed: Appropriate containers, florist oasis, scissors, toothpicks, 6" skewers, lemon, galox or ivy leaves, fresh seasonal fruit and large wedges of cheese.

Step 1: Select an appropriate container remembering that overall height of centerpiece should be 1-1/2 times the container height.

Step 2: Fill the container with water soaked oasis. Add additional blocks of oasis as necessary to attain proper height and secure blocks together with skewers.

Step 4: Place 3 skewers in the bottom of a pineapple and position in center of display.

Step 5: If using cheese, secure wedges to pineapple and oasis using skewers.

Step 6: If using only fruit, select larger pieces such as papaya or grapefruit. Position fruit around edge of container. Secure with skewers into oasis.

Step 7: Place skewers into base of other fruits and arrange by securing into pineapple or oasis.

Step 8: Select well-formed clusters of grapes and fill in around fruit using skewers and toothpicks to secure. Use strawberries, if available, to fill in.

Step 9: Tuck leaves around fruit to produce a natural look.

Step 10: Check all sides for uniformity and balance. (These arrangements can be done the day before — wrapped tightly and refrigerated.)

Step 11: Step back, congratulate yourself, and wait for all your guests' accolades.

Pub Lunch at Portobello

BILL of FARE

**Pub Lunch
at Portobello**

---

*Grilled Cornish Game Birds
with Citrus Glaze*

Pork and Lamb Pastie

The Innkeepers' Tomatoes

*Veggie Lunch with
Fresh Herbed Mayonnaise*

Portobello Market has detractors as well as devotees among travel writers, but in our opinion, no self-respecting antique hunter should be in London on a Saturday morning without making an appearance at this world famous street market at least by 9 a.m. On a warm summer Saturday, 7 a.m. is not too early to get a jump on the international throng of tourist/treasure hunters who will fight the local spike-haired youths for strolling space along the two blocks of Portobello Road on either side of Westbourne Grove. (Fortunately, most of these colorful folk are there to see and be seen among the rows of stalls and have little interest in the real antique action.) There are some good buys to be had in the street stalls if you get there

Old pewter, hunting trophies and game paintings have graced the paneled walls of English pubs for hundreds of years. While we remain sensitive to the critical need to protect endangered species, we nevertheless recognize the many facts of life that were different in the 18th and 19th centuries when the wearers of the horns and skins commonly found in antique shops and pubs met their fate. Pub chairs such as this Broad-arm Windsor have increased in price dramatically over the past 10 years — since collectors and designers found what pub crawlers always knew — that these high-backed country pieces are handsome, durable and extremely comfortable — particularly well suited to long hours of serious conversation over a few pints of lager.

1. A and 1. B: Pair of similar English Ash and Elm Broad-arm Windsor Chairs with Christmas Tree Back Splat, c. 1850; 2. English Queen Anne Oak Dropleaf Gateleg Table, c. 1720; 3. English Queen Anne Oak Corner Settle with Paneled Back and Cabriole Legs, c. 1710;

early enough, but most antiques are in the shops and the arcades in the buildings behind the stalls.

As parking is almost impossible around Portobello, take a cab, and don't forget your umbrella or your shopping bags. You will need breakfast as well as lunch at Portobello if you get the early start that we recommend. One of the first markets to open, about 7 a.m., is Roger's Arcade at the top end of the road (on the right as you walk up). Upstairs, there is a food stall with a few tables and benches that is good for croissant and coffee (or a full English breakfast if you can spare the shopping time). English silver, antique jewelry, brass candlesticks, Staffordshire figures and writing boxes are good buys in this crowded arcade, but one sees every sort of small including nauticals and fine Oriental porcelain.

Halfway down this same block is Van's Arcade, once an individually owned source of 15th-17th century architectural and carved wood classics, but now a multi-stall arcade, where many of the current dealers specialize in the same sort of rare early pieces. There are similar multi-room, multi-level arcades/markets on the west side of Portobello Road and a few on the east side extending down to the food stalls at the lower end of this 2-block area, and on both sides of Westbourne Grove in the block west of Portobello. It would take a dozen Saturdays to investigate properly each labyrinth of stalls and, as the dealers change spaces and the markets do not specialize, it is not practical to try to direct a buyer to any particular source.

The previously recommended *Guide to the Antique Shops* does include some of these arcades and may be a help getting started, but the best way to approach Portobello is to go early, quickly cover the street stalls before the crowds gather, then wander in several of the arcades to get a feel for the kind of item they stock — some are heavily into jewelry, some into prints, others porcelain, etc. Choose to look or move on, keeping in mind that the best buys in a market (or a shop) are the items the specialist does not normally handle but has had to buy in order to get the other items he does want. For example, a porcelain dealer may have an excellent 16th century Flemish walnut wood carving in his stall which he would like to dispose of quickly because it's not his forte. When you do find something you are interested in — before deciding to move on and keep looking — get the best price from the dealer and then ask yourself how disappointed you will be to return and find it sold. Very often another buyer is lingering in the next stall just waiting for you to put the piece down so he or she can pounce on it.

If you are really uncertain about a purchase and not just delaying the inevitable, make a note of the piece, stall number, market name or number and be sure to find out

4. Table accessories include Pewter Ale Mugs, Candlesticks and an unusual Covered Vegetable Platter with engraved Coat of Arms; 5. English Tole Tea Cannister, 19th C., converted to lamp base; 6. English Painted Iron "Carriage" Door Stop, c. 1900; 7. Scottish Painted Iron Umbrella Stand, c. 1840, with various 19th C. Walking Sticks; 8. Pillows made from fragments of worn-out Oriental carpets — an effective way to recycle antiques; 9. Primitive English Game Painting, 19th C.; 10. English Genre Painting of a team patiently waiting outside the pub, 19th C.; 11. Collection of 19th C. English Pewter, all having raised (repoussé) armorial decoration.

London Antique Fairs

In addition to the famous annual Grosvenor House Antique Fair, held every year in early June, there are several other annual and semi-annual fairs of major interest — Chelsea, Olympia, City of London, West London and the new "antiques and decoratives" fairs. The latter reflect the intense current interest in English interior design with the admission of highly decorative "later" pieces along with the period antiques.

The staggering number of weekend fairs in the hotels of central London and in the suburbs forces one to choose two or three of the most convenient ones. Jewelry, silverware, Staffordshire, brass candlesticks and other smalls are the focus, but dealers come in from all over England and bring everything with them except large furniture. You need to bring pounds, as converting U.S. dollars — bills or traveler's checks — is a bother for both buyer and seller. The "fresh" merchandise attracts many London and international dealers, so price negotiation is expected.

what time the dealer will close. By the end of the day, each place looks like every other so make the same notations if you purchase something and plan to return to pick it up. Do not miss the fine individual shops located in the area that are open other days of the week as well, but which seem to always have fresh stock for Saturdays. There are some excellent sources for Georgian and earlier furniture here.

In Portobello, as at Bermondsey, it is a good idea to keep an eye out for the highly decorative piece that may not be very old but which is uniquely English. These treasures may be carved wood, embroidered fabric, toy or tool, startling or just strange. The common denominator is unusual and decorative. As prices for period pieces and early repros fly beyond the pocket's reach for so many would-be collectors, these pieces are a solace and are available at fairly modest prices in most markets. But even these esoterica, ephemera, etc. are catching on and entire shows are now developing around the "antiques and decoratives" theme. So, move quickly.

Portobello is a good market for Oriental ceramics (particularly Imari) and antique hand painted English prints but there are plenty of fakes and restorations about, so do query dealers concerning age and condition. In England, if your questions are specific, you can generally get a specific answer and rely on it. If the answer is an equivocation, i.e. "The piece is just as I bought it", keep looking. (Warning: ceramics with cracks, repaired or not, are supposed to respond with a dull plunk when ticked with a finger — but we are told that now some experts can repair and retain the clear ring of a perfect piece.)

There are more transient treasures at Portobello too...the craggy-faced organ grinder with his scavenger monkey...the strong man who always manages to escape the impossible tangle of chain and locks...the musicians

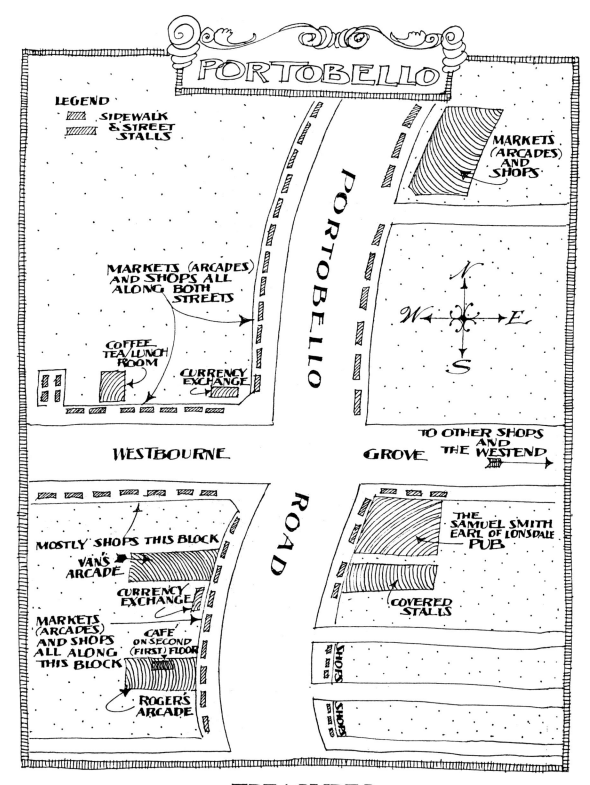

TREASURES

Portobello Market — London (West)

Every Saturday. 7 a.m. to 4 p.m. (approximately)

Corner Portobello Road and Westbourne Grove

Indoor London Markets

All markets feature the full range of smalls with many specialist dealers in porcelain, silver, jewelry, fabrics, Deco and Nouveau, and most are open every day but Sunday.

Grays Antique Markets
*58 Davies Street, W1
Within walking distance of Mayfair hotels…something for everyone (except large furniture) in two buildings.*

Bond Street Antique Center
*124 New Bond Street, W1
Principally jewelry and silver with some porcelain and paintings. Near the auction houses, many fine art/antique galleries and Gray's Markets.*

Alfies Market *(see facing paragraph)*

Antiquarius, Chelsea and Chenil Galleries *131-141, 253 and 181-183 Kings Road. All interesting (listed in order of our preference) with some furniture, paintings, early fabrics, wood carvings, antique books and books on antiques. The addresses seem closer than they are, but it's possible and interesting to walk from one to the other. Each has a small café.*

of dubious but delightful talents…and the pub on the corner. There are other pubs in the market area, but the "Samuel Smith, Earl of Lonsdale" pub on the corner of Portobello Road and Westbourne Grove is the place where, if you stay long enough, you will see someone you know from back home along with a few thousand other colorful characters. More importantly, the pub food is, according to our frequent taste tests, among the best of its kind in London. Order a half-pint of lager or cider, maneuver your way through the crowd to a table which someone else must hold while you return to the food bar for big broiled bangers with potato salad, cottage pie, Scotch eggs and other fresh, homemade, delicious traditional English pub fare (and be sure to help yourself to the chutney, pickles and mustard). Another experience for your treasure collection.

After lunch, check out the shops in the blocks along Westbourne Grove just east of Portobello or stop by Alfies Market (Tuesday-Saturday, 10 a.m.-6 p.m.) at 13-25 Church Street on your way back to the West End. This maze of shops in a huge multi-story building has too much Nouveau, Deco, and clothes to be a favorite stop for us, but we have found some good, early wood carvings, small tables, and Vienna bronzes which can make the trip worthwhile.

On to Camden Passage

The other major Saturday (and Wednesday) market is Camden Passage in Islington on the other (east) side of London. We often go there after Portobello, sometimes missing the outdoor stalls which shut down by 4 p.m. (earlier if the weather is bad). Camden Passage is a charming three block village of permanent shops, some of which are open daily and some only on market days plus several

arcades of small stalls open just on Wednesdays and Saturdays. The shops feature English pine, early copper, Georgian Mahogany, and Country French (and often have some of the most interesting and decorative antiques you'll see anywhere in England).

If your London Saturday will not accommodate two markets, choose Portobello. If you are in London on a Wednesday, you can do both shops and stalls at Camden Passage then or take a chance on finding enough shops open on another weekday. When you do go, have a hearty lunch of "Bubble and Squeak" at the pub on the east end of the passage or, if you can spare the time from antiquing, indulge in the 4-course luncheons at one of the more fashionable cafés. Each of these principal London markets — Bermondsey, Portobello and Camden Passage — has its own pluses, personality and possibilities which bring us back again and again, year after year.

The Innkeepers' Tomatoes

Early spring and summer farmers' markets are eagerly awaited for the best in fresh fruits, vegetables, and herbs. Tomatoes are especially versatile — whether just sliced and splashed with a vinaigrette, grilled or broiled as in this recipe. They add color and taste to almost any menu.

Mix together:
1/2 C. goat cheese
1/4 C. Parmesan cheese
1/2 C. cream cheese
2 T. minced scallions

Sauté (then squeeze dry and mince):
1 lb. fresh spinach
2 T. butter
1/2 clove garlic
pinch basil
pinch tarragon

Choose small to medium size farm fresh tomatoes. Hollow tomatoes, lightly salt and turn over to drain. Turn drained tomato upright and sprinkle inside with tarragon and minced basil — just a pinch. Layer spinach first and then cheese on top — approximately 1/2 and 1/2. Bake at 400 degrees for 15 minutes.

Grilled Cornish Game Hen, Citrus Glaze

These game hens are very moist and a beautiful mahogany color because of the hickory chips. You can use this same glaze on chicken breast or quail, and they are just as good at room temperature.

Fresh Game Hens
3 dried apricots
2 T. butter
1/4 tsp. orange zest
lemon wedge

Apricot Glaze:
4 oz. apricot jelly
4 oz. orange marmalade
zest of 1 lemon, grated
1/2 stick butter
salt & pepper

Clean and dry game hen. Stuff with apricots, butter, orange zest and lemon wedge. Place over medium coals topped with hickory soaked chips. Cover lightly and turn every 10 to 15 minutes until a mahogany color — about 40 minutes. Brush with glaze and put in low oven, covered for 20 minutes or until serving time.

Apricot Glaze — blend together apricot jelly, orange marmalade, grated zest of lemon and butter in medium saucepan and taste for seasoning.

Pork and Lamb Pasties

Although traditional pastie crust is quite firm, this is a very flaky version and can be filled with thick, hearty stew made with red wine and loads of fresh herbs.

Pastry:
1-3/4 C. flour
pinch of salt
3/4 stick of butter
2 T. lard
4-6 T. cold water

Sift flour and salt into bowl. Add butter and lard and cut into a cornmeal texture. Make a well in the center, add cold water and stir until it makes a soft dough — refrigerate for at least 1 hour. Roll out and cut 4" to 8" circles. May be frozen and used when needed.

Filling (layer on 1/2 of pastry):
sliced parsnips, steamed
sliced red onion
2 medium potatoes, sliced
1/2 lb. pork, coarsely
  chopped by hand
1/2 lb. lamb, coarsely
  chopped by hand
2 minced garlic cloves
fresh sprigs of
  rosemary & tarragon
pinch of thyme & rosemary
salt & freshly ground pepper
dot of butter
pinch of mace

Place filling in center of pastry. Fold over, brush with beaten egg, and crimp edges. Brush with beaten egg and 1 tablespoon water and place on greased baking sheet. Bake at 350 degrees for 40 minutes or until brown.

Tea in the Georgian City

BILL *of* FARE

Georgian Tea

Miniature Gammon Scones

*Devonshire Pears wrapped
in Pastry*

Avocado and Brie Bits

Red Radish and Egg Brioche

Watercress Radicchio Squares

Almond Puffs

Morecamb Bay Shrimp Butter

*Miniature Mincemeat Tart
Kentish Cherry Tart
Lemon Curd Tart*

Hot Berry Tea, Bristol Sherry

A one-day train trip to Bath is a must for the English antique hunter, and overnight in one of the magnificent Georgian homes which have been converted to hotels is even better. The Wednesday morning market at Guinea Lane is one of the best provincial (meaning outside of London) markets in England and draws plenty of London dealers with the possibility of "new" material from West England and Wales. On four cramped floors of an old church near the city's hotel center, Guinea Lane offers the full range of smalls and a few furniture pieces that just might be the bargain of the year. At times we go early (6:30 a.m.) to the market for a couple of hours, return to the hotel to enjoy our 'included' full English breakfast,

If asked to name the most widely recognized tradition of England, most of us would probably say, "afternoon tea." Some of us who have trouble enough with the calories in three meals a day feel fortunate to have been spared the tradition of a fourth...filled with all the irresistible riches of the kitchen, but for a truly elegant occasion, an English tea is hard to beat. Similarly, Georgian furniture is hard to beat...and is high on every collector's "most widely recognized" list.

1. English Chippendale Mahogany Dropleaf, Gateleg Dining Table, c. 1770; 2. Chinese Imperial Yellow Porcelain Garden Seat, c. 1800; 3. English Rosewood Tea Caddy inlaid with Mother-of-Pearl, c. 1820; 4. Turkish Carpet, 20th C.; 5. Pair of English Chinoiserie (in the Chinese style) side chairs made in the Queen Anne style, c. 1790; 6. English Chippendale Mahogany Chest of Drawers on splayed bracket feet, c. 1780; 7. English Mahogany Knife Box, c. 1780; 8. Chinese Brass Jardinaire, c. 1840; 9. English 18th C.

then head back to Guinea Lane, the nearby shops and other markets.

More often, we enjoy the fare at the little coffee shop in Guinea Lane or the larger one in the close by Great Western Antiques Center. The stalls at Great Western, featuring furniture of every period, are open daily and augmented on Wednesdays by a large market in the basement. There are some excellent small shops in the area that open early with fresh goods (usually country) on Wednesday and two other small weekly markets. Once again, you can use your *Guide to the Antique Shops* rather than wander up and down the streets (some of these are quite steep).

Within an easy walk away from the markets,

toward Bath center, are several elegant shops which open at 10 a.m. or so and specialize in fine Georgian furniture and accessories. Since a visit to this city is not complete without a tour of the remarkable Roman Baths you may wish to combine this archeological treasure hunt with afternoon tea in the adjacent Pump Room. (While we suggest tea, we never take time from our too-brief Wednesday in Bath for more than a quick bite in the markets or one of the pubs. If we did take the time out, it would be to have the buffet lunch in one of Bath's most famous restaurants, The Hole in the Wall, that happens to be right down the block from Great Western.)

You can day trip to Bath via fast train or take advantage of the many good hotels which are close enough to the antique markets and shops for you to spend Tuesday night and walk to the treasures early on Wednesday morning. If you brave the left lane and drive down on the super-fast M4 from London (or take the leisurely route through the Cotswolds), you will want to browse the shops on Bath's London Road (you may also visit them via cab on your way back to the train station) while venturing on to one of England's most picturesque villages, Castle Combe. There are a few antique shops there, but the treasures are the village itself and the Manor House, now an exceptionally attractive country house hotel with a good bar for a late afternoon picker-upper after a hard day in the markets.

You will enjoy the trip to Bath, but you need not leave London to acquire Georgian furniture. Much of the best appears at the major auction houses and in the world-famous shops on Bond and Regent Streets, as well as in shops near Grosvenor Square and at both ends of the King's Road. The 18th century is considered by most to be the high point in the design and crafting of English

handpainted Bird Print;
10. English Chinoiserie lacquer fire surround; 11. English Mahogany Tea Caddy, c. 1770; 12. Pair English Brass "Beehive" Candlesticks, c. 1860; 13. English Seascape, oil on canvas, 19th C.; 14. English Mahogany Tallcase Clock with broken pediment arch, c. 1780; 15. Reproduction Chippendale style Wing Chair; 16. Miscellaneous English Porcelain, Pressed Glass and Silverplate Serving Pieces, c. 1880-1920.

Guinea Lane Market — Bath
Every Wednesday, 6:00 a.m. to 2:00 p.m. (approximately). End of Guinea Lane off Lansdown Road.

Three Worthwhile Day Trips Out of London

Brighton: *Take the train from Victoria (frequent departures) to Brighton Station. You can walk to the Lanes, the narrow cobblestone passageways between the central shopping streets and the sea (ask directions from any native). Once you find one of the many shops you can ask for a map to the others. While in the area, take an hour to tour the famous Royal Pavillion. Hail a taxi for Upper North Street where you can see two full blocks of interesting shops for a couple of hours before catching another cab back to the station.*

The shops feature good early furniture — lots of English and a little French — but all of them have choice smalls if that is your preference.

Petworth and Arundel, West Sussex: *Two charming neighbor villages (located southwest of Gatwick) that are filled with good antique shops and pubs. Petworth also boasts an important National Trust manor — Petworth House — and Arundel lies in the shadow of a splendid castle. Each of these properties is a treasure*

furniture, and there is a surprisingly large amount of George I, II and III furniture still in evidence outside museums to prove the point. Incidentally, don't let the sophisticated look of the quality English shops scare you off. In these days when some collectors wish to do their collecting conspicuously in public, you often find that the prices in the stately shops compare favorably with the prices being fetched at auction.

Still, attending a London auction provides you with a free, advanced course in antique collecting and should be pursued. The Monday *Telegraph* and the *Antiques Gazette* (available for sale in many of the London markets) provide a weekly listing of major sales. Phillips Auction House has several good general sales each week which we prefer over the more frenetic specialty sales held at Sothebys and Christies. However, all three auction houses are in the same West End neighborhood, so you can preview several sales and reach your own conclusion.

For best results, preview an auction carefully prior to the day the sale is held, checking in the catalog the pieces that interest you. Note the auction company's description of each piece as well as the estimate of value, and compare both with any judgment you may have. If you intend to be a bidder, write down (or keep firmly in mind) the maximum amount you will bid, and then recheck your initial impression by previewing again the day of the sale. Regardless of whether you intend to bid, follow closely the bidding with respect to those items you have checked and jot down the amount of each successful bid. (If you cannot stay for the sale, you can arrange to have the results mailed to you. You can also arrange to leave a bid which the auction house will execute for you when the auctioneer reaches your piece.) You may find that you can buy at auction. There is always the chance that those present are ignoring a piece that interests you. The mechanics of bidding are much the same at each house — register, get a number and bid quickly and obviously on your choices. A subtle motion from a new, unknown bidder may or may not be noticed until too late. But even if you do not succeed in buying, you will have learned a lot about value in one of the simplest and most effective ways.

Another way to learn value is to shop the world-class shops. After the initial sticker shock, remind yourself that these people are in business and want to sell this fabulous furniture. Therefore, if you have a sincere interest in a piece, the dealer will not be offended if you ask about the "price for export." He will certainly remove the VAT (Value Added Tax) from your price and your question allows the dealer to come down in price for other reasons, if possible. However, you should not be offended if the dealer says, "I'm sorry but I really can't take less. I'm not able to replace the piece even for what I am asking." Period furniture in good condition is so rare in England now that reasonable prices become obsolete quickly.

Of course, you need not leave London for tea either. A day in the auction houses can be enervating, even if you don't buy a thing, and you may require a lift about now. Since you are already in the neighborhood, you have a good excuse to fortify yourself with the uncompromising quality and calories in the sandwiches, cakes and chocolates that accompany tea in the venerable Fortnum & Masons. The whole store is a treasure. Forget your diet and enjoy!

trove worthy of your attention. (Please check current open times before making your trip plans.) The shops in Petworth are up and down and all around; get a map in your first stop. Arundel has fewer shops, mostly around the square. Both towns feature multiple dealer antique markets. Easiest transport is driving, hiring a car and driver, or working out a train/ taxi schedule.

Windsor-Eton: *You have probably been here to see the castle and the boy's school; if not, you will want to include them on your day trip itinerary. Across the Thames from each other, the castle and school have all the great traditions of England plus lots of antique markets and shops and several good restaurants.*

Take a train (or boat) to Windsor — visit the shops on that side of the river — have lunch Thames side and cross the bridge to the long main street of shops in Eton. There are enough handsomely dressed school boys about to give the proper "old school" flavor to the place.

Devonshire Pears Wrapped in Pastry

These pears look much more difficult to prepare than they are. The presentation is very pretty and the natural flavors heavenly. The taste can be changed by poaching the pears in red wine and using just the crème anglaise for sauce.

Pears:

Peel 6 pears and leave stems on
1 bottle White Zinfandel
2 sticks cinnamon
1 whole vanilla bean
1/4 C. sugar
1/2 tsp. nutmeg

Filling:

8 oz. cream cheese
grated zest of 1 orange
1 tsp. vanilla
2 T. powdered sugar
1 T. dry sherry

Poach pear in liquid until fork tender. Cool overnight in liquid. Drain pears. Cut pear in half — being careful not to lose the stem. Core and fill hollow with sherry mixture. Fit pear back together (can toothpick it until crust is in place) and place on a square of puff pastry. Bring the pastry up and around pear using it as a form and then bring "leaves" down on the side. This pastry will slide down so keep it up at the very top. Brush pastry with egg wash and refrigerate 1 hour. Bake at 400 degrees for 15 minutes or until brown.

Crème Anglaise:

Whisk: 8 egg yolks and
*   1 C. sugar*
Heat until boiling: 1 qt.
*   heavy cream*
vanilla bean
zest of 1 orange

Heat yolks and sugar until warm in double boiler. Whisk hot cream into mixture drop by drop on very low heat. Strain and set it over ice — fold in small amount of orange zest.

Raspberry Sauce:

4 C. frozen raspberries,
*   thawed*
1/2 C. powdered sugar
1 T. Kirsch
1/2 tsp. vanilla

Put all ingredients in food processor and process until smooth. Taste to adjust the sweetness.

Avocado and Brie Bits

These little sandwiches are so creamy and rich — just right for tea time. You might like to add a smoked ham (thinly sliced) to make them more substantial.

Thin slices of pumpernickel bread, avocado and brie cheese
1-2 C. minced arugula

Honey mustard:
1/2 C. Dijon mustard
1/4 C. honey
1-1/2 C. salad oil
2 T. shallots
1/2 C. white wine vinegar

Whisk the mustard, honey, oil, shallots and vinegar together — adjust if it is too sweet for you. Coat one side of pumpernickel with honey mustard. Layer with 1/8" slices of brie and avocado. Top with pumpernickel slice and cut into triangles. Lightly coat sides of sandwich with honey mustard and roll sides in minced arugula.

Watercress and Radicchio Squares

There can be so many sweet things at a tea that the tart contrast of these squares can be appealing. They may be made open-faced also.

sliced firm white bread
2 T. horseradish
1 C. mayonnaise
1 tsp. Dijon mustard (optional)
2 C. watercress, minced
2 C. radicchio, minced

Cut firm white bread into squares. Lightly coat square with a horseradish and mayonnaise mixture. (May also add a touch of mustard.) Mince watercress and radicchio. Sprinkle it on top of one slice, top with another and then lightly coat edges with horseradish mayonnaise and roll in chopped watercress.

Shrimp Butter

This butter is delicious on warm biscuits or crackers as an appetizer.

2-1/2 lb. shrimp, boiled, deveined
6 T. butter
3-1/2 T. mayonnaise
1/2 tsp. lemon juice
pinch of mace
1 tsp. Worcestershire sauce
2-3 drops tabasco
salt & pepper

In food processor process shrimp until finely minced. Add butter, mayonnaise and spices. Process until rather smooth. Chill and serve with warm biscuits or crackers.

Almond Puffs

This is a very tender and delicious bread that is versatile and virtually fail proof.
I make this in 8" rolls and bake for Christmas morning gifts to neighbors. They may
be prepared at least one week in advance and frozen.

Bread dough:

2 pkg. dry yeast
1/2 C. warm water
2 eggs
4 C. flour
1 C. sour cream
1/2 C. sugar
1 tsp. salt
1/2 C. butter, melted
slivered almonds

Filling (mix together in
food processor):

24 oz. cream cheese, softened
1 C. sugar
3 eggs, beaten
1/8 tsp. salt
2 tsp. almond extract
1 tsp. vanilla

Glaze (mix together):

2 C. powdered sugar
4 T. Half and Half
1 tsp. vanilla
1 tsp. almond extract

Sprinkle 2 packages dry yeast over warm water. Stir to dissolve the yeast. Warm sour cream with sugar, salt and butter until the sugar is dissolved. Stir in the melted butter and then let mixture return to room temperature. Add 2 eggs, sour cream mixture and yeast to 4 C. flour. Stir until all the flour is incorporated. Cover tightly and let rise until double — 2-4 hours — or cover and refrigerate overnight. Divide dough into 2 parts and roll out into 9" x 11" rectangle. This dough will feel almost like cookie dough. Cut dough into 4" square. Spread layer of cream cheese filling and 1/2 tsp. slivered almonds on top. Fold in half and then over again into squares. Pinch dough together around all sides. Let rise until double again and bake at 375 degrees for 12-15 minutes. Frost with glaze and roll in toasted slivered almonds.

Miniature Mincemeat Tarts

Vegetable mincemeats are lighter than a meat-based mincemeat, and because this recipe is made with tomatillos it will be somewhat spicier.

Pâté Brisée *(see index)*

Tomatillo Mincemeat:

20 tomatillos, cored and
    chopped
Salt
1 orange
4 C. Granny Smith apples
2 C. seedless raisins
1-1/2 C. chopped suet
3 — 3-1/2 C. brown sugar
1/4 C. cider vinegar
2 tsp. cinnamon
1 tsp. cloves
1 tsp. freshly grated nutmeg
1/2 tsp. freshly minced ginger
1/4 C. rum

Sprinkle salt on chopped tomatillos and let stand 1 hour. Drain the tomatillos and cover with boiling water. Let stand 10 minutes and then drain. Zest orange and chop pulp. Mix the orange and tomatillos together in a heavy saucepan. Add remaining ingredients and cook over medium-low heat until boiling. Adjust the seasonings and pour into hot sterilized jars. Seal jars and process in a water bath for 15 minutes.

Prepare Pâté Brisée (see index) and line miniature tart pans with dough. Refrigerate for 30 minutes and fill with tomatillo mincemeat. Bake at 375 degrees for 15-20 minutes or until crust is golden. Let cool.

Cherry Tarts

The combination of a buttery crust, sweet filling and tart cherries is delicious.

Shortbread Shell:

1-1/3 C. salted butter, soft
1 C. superfine sugar
2 C. flour
1/2 tsp. baking powder
Pinch of salt

Cheese and Cherry Filling:

8 oz. cream cheese, room
    temperature
1/8 tsp. almond flavoring
Powdered sugar to sweeten
1 T. vanilla yogurt
Sliced almonds
1 lb. fresh cherries, pitted
Red currant jelly
Amaretto

Place butter, sugar, flour, baking powder and salt in work bowl of mixer and slowly beat until it forms a dough. Place in plastic wrap and refrigerate for at least 1 hour. Roll dough to 1/4" thickness and press into 6 miniature pans. Bake in 350-degree oven until browned (approximately 15 minutes). Let cool and remove gently.

Mix cream cheese, almond flavoring, yogurt, and powdered sugar together. Taste cherries to see how sweet they are and then adjust sweetness in the cream cheese mixture. Spread cheese mixture generously on bottom of shell. Sprinkle almonds on top. Place whole cherries on top of almonds. Melt jelly with Amaretto and brush this glaze over cherry topping. Refrigerate for 1 hour before serving.

A Regency Theatre Supper

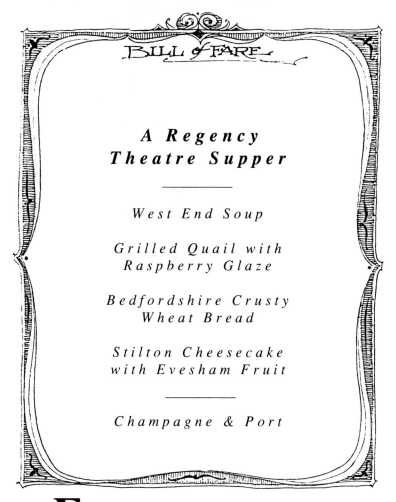

BILL of FARE

**A Regency
Theatre Supper**

West End Soup

_Grilled Quail with
Raspberry Glaze_

_Bedfordshire Crusty
Wheat Bread_

_Stilton Cheesecake
with Evesham Fruit_

Champagne & Port

For many collectors, the interest in English furniture begins and ends with the 18th century. What about the 200 years before and since? What is desirable and what is still available from those years either in England or the United States? The following is a hunter's viewpoint.

There was not much furniture in England or elsewhere during the Renaissance. Castle furnishings were few, simple and portable and consisted of long tables, benches and boxes or coffers — all made of oak. Some fine Tudor/Elizabethan pieces have survived the centuries, but most now grace museums. The 16th century pieces in today's market are either priced for millionaires or merit close scrutiny for massive reconstruction.

English Regency is, frankly, not our favorite period. We have had some classic examples with brass and giltwood in all the right places, but not for this photography session. However, we think this 1. elegant secretary/bookcase, while missing the fancy trim, nevertheless effectively illustrates in scale and construction that transition period between Georgian and Victorian furniture. The ram's heads cresting the cabriole legs of the 2. late 19th C. Wing Chair are a motif we would have preferred to show on a period Regency piece — but such is the luck of treasure hunters!

3. English Mahogany Barometer, c. 1800; 4. English Mason's Ironstone Tureen, Plates and Bowls; 5. Pair of English Brass Cathedral Sticks with reeded columns, c. 1830; 6. English Silverplate Champagne Cooler, c. 1870; 7. Pair English Staffordshire Lions, c. 1870.

The 17th century offers better hunting opportunities. Simple Jacobean oak tables are in the shops, some in surprisingly original condition at relatively reasonable prices (far more reasonable than same-period joynt [joined] stools which have reached nonsensical prices if presumed to be original). Welsh dressers and dresser bases of the 17th century are seen at extremely high prices (over $20,000), but the choice ones may justify the tag, and they will not get cheaper. (Most dressers and dresser bases are later — early to mid 18th century — but even these are scarce and expensive now.)

Charles II chairs, though fragile and for decorative use only, often appear at very fair prices (so do 19th century repros, so check carefully). Late 17th century William & Mary chests are often available in shops and at auctions, most in oak with some of the "new" walnut beginning to show up as ornamental veneers.

Our best 17th-century-English luck was a small oak credence table, completely original, in a U.S. garage sale for $1.50. Dealers may scoff, but it **was** the real thing — so hunters, take heart. Another local estate discovery was a museum quality 17th century paneled oak coffer. Such finds in our country are not so surprising when one recalls the major turn-of-the-century exodus of Americans on the Grand Tour of Europe. They found an abundance of fine early furniture for sale to a strong dollar and shipped some choice lots back home.

Moving on to the early 18th century, Queen Anne still offers possibilities. A few years ago, we were elated to find an original walnut dressing stool in a Bath market for 100 pounds ($185). Just recently, two period Queen Anne chairs and an important period walnut bureau bookcase changed local owners through our shop. Those treasures had journeyed from England to New York around 1900, and then to Kansas City in 1960. The point is there are good pieces of Queen Anne furniture on the market. They seem overpriced at auction (even in wretched condition), expensive but still worth the money in English shops…and great bargains in the markets or estate sales, especially in the U.S., if you know what you are looking for and have a bit of luck.

Once upon a time, when all antique furniture collectors lived in châteaux, manors or mansions in Western Europe and the United States, periods went in and out of favor. Only museums wanted 17th and 18th century oak: William & Mary was too fussy for some, Queen Anne was too plain, late Georgian was too fragile, Regency was too French and Victorian was ignored. But Chippendale, in all its mahogany glory, was a magic word; then and now. The difference is that now collectors live in Iowa farm houses and Park Avenue condos…in Arabian tents and Kyoto cottages…and challenge each other in the sale rooms for the limited number of antiques from every period and every place. All early furniture is in demand, but Chippendale is still the magic word in at least 13 languages. These tables, chairs and desks that were crafted during the last half of the 18th century command the attention and purse of the serious collector to such a degree that the English market buyer is excited to find even a wormy country chair that is "of the period."

Less of a force but still a factor is the late 18th century furniture crafted according to the designs of George Hepplewhite and Thomas Sheraton. From the lavish rococo embellishments of Chippendale, the taste of the times turned to the clean, neo-classic lines of Hepplewhite and the similar but more feminine approach of Sheraton, which remained popular through the end of the century, closing out the Georgian period.

As indicated, it can be worthwhile to hunt for 18th century English furniture in the United States. After all, since the week World War II was over in Europe, American dealers have been importing weekly container loads of English antiques. Products of the 18th century were the goal, and there are now, literally, tons of fine Georgian furniture in this country. Much of the best is, and will remain, in museums and private collections but the double nemesis of death and divorce results in a constant recirculation of the remaining pieces.

Furniture from the short Regency period, a dramatic transition between late Georgian and early Victorian with a strong Napoleonic influence, is recognized by its sleek, almost severe style featuring highly figured

woods with gilding, brass inlay and ormolu mounts. The occasional pieces of "real" Regency that appear in the sale rooms and shops are coveted by up-scale interior designers and bring very high prices. Some less glamourous Regency furniture — really streamlined versions of Georgian styles — is available and more reasonable.

There is general agreement that the golden age of furniture died when Queen Victoria's reign began, the fault of the Industrial Revolution, not of the Queen. Still, some of the most popular country furniture is from this period; such treasures as pine dressers, cricket tables, Broadarm Windsor pub chairs, and oak plank top farm tables. These are still available but getting harder to find and more expensive each day. Certainly the smaller arts and crafts flourished during the 19th century. Most of the antique brass candlesticks, copper sauce pans and molds, potteries and porcelains, silver and silverplate that are around and affordable today were produced in prodigious quantities by Victorian craftsmen.

Formal furniture, however, becomes larger, heavier, and curvier from 1840 onwards, and, with the exception of some hand-carved ornament, made by machine. In large supply with little demand, these Victorian pieces are still quite reasonable. Edwardian furniture of the late 19th/early 20th century is characteristically copied from Hepplewhite styles with elaborate inlay on mahogany. The "shipping goods" that are imported in bulk to the United States and sold in warehouses to the unwary or unconcerned customers as "antiques" consist largely of this mass-produced Edwardian "hotel furniture" — wardrobes, bed frames, night stands and desks — plus a sprinkling of late Victorian hall trees and brass beds. A hunt for these pieces is not necessary as they jump out everywhere and are not of interest to serious antique collectors.

Of more significance is the turn-of-the-century furniture of the Arts and Crafts movement and Art Nouveau/Art Deco schools. All are collectible and often costly now. Whether or not they should ever be termed "antique" is a subject suitable for late night discussion.

Such friendly controversies over what is becoming or will ultimately become an antique should take place over a supper of seafood soup and spinach soufflé accompanied by a crisp European Chardonnay — preferably at Langan's Brasserie, near Berkeley Square, on a Thursday evening in early November, creating the perfect prelude to one more thrilling Friday morning treasure hunt at our beloved Bermondsey Market.

Grilled Quail with Raspberry Glaze

European boneless quail are very easy to grill ahead and then gently rewarm, basting with the glaze. Unstuffed, they are great the next morning for breakfast.

4 boneless European style quail
2 C. Beaujolais
2 T. minced shallots
1/2 tsp. minced rosemary
4 T. butter
1/2 C. fresh or frozen raspberries
1/4 C. chicken stock
1/4 C. Half and Half

Stuffing:
2 C. wheat bread, cubed, dried
2 T. onions sautéed in butter
1 tsp. rosemary
1/4 C. raspberries
2 whole eggs
1 tsp. orange zest
1/2 C. chicken stock
salt & pepper
1/4 C. finely minced pecan
1/4 C. finely minced celery

Reduce Beaujolais to 1/2 C. with 2 tablespoons shallots and spices. Add stock and cream. Reduce until very thick. Add butter 1 tablespoon at a time and whisk in until fully incorporated. Remove from heat. Fill quail cavities with stuffing and sew up end or toothpick opening closed. Immediately before serving, add raspberries.

Sear quail over hot coals on both sides (2-3 minutes per side). Remove to baking dish, brush with reduction sauce. Cover tightly with foil. Bake in oven for 20-40 minutes. Baste every 10 minutes. Right before serving add fresh raspberries and pass the sauce separately.

West End Soup

Every time we make this soup in Le Picnique people rave about the flavors. The cider makes it both rich and very mild.

1 T. minced garlic
4 lb. red and yellow onions,
    thinly sliced
3/4 lb. butter
1/3 C. flour
9 C. beef stock
9 C. chicken stock
1 C. dry white wine
3 C. apple cider
3 bay leaves
1-1/2 T. dried thyme

Sauté garlic and onions in 3/4 lb. butter until they are translucent, then add flour. Stir until the flour is equally distributed and cook for 5 minutes. Add remaining ingredients and simmer for 1 hour. Place garlicky croutons topped with Gruyere cheese in hot soup.

Crusty Whole Grain Bread

Nothing tastes better than homemade whole grain bread. It is a nice Sunday afternoon task that brings rave reviews all week long. This recipe can be made with either rye, wheat flour, or a combination of the two.

1 pkg. active dry yeast
1/4 C. warm water
2-/4 C. warm water
1 egg, beaten
1/2 C. melted butter
1-1/2 tsp. salt
1/2 C. honey
4 C. whole grain flour, wheat or rye
4 C. all purpose flour

Stir yeast into 1/4 C. warm water and allow it to rest for 10 minutes. Beat together 2-1/4 C. warm water, egg, butter, salt and honey. Add this mixture to the yeast mixture. Mix thoroughly and then add all but 1/2 C. of flour to mixture. Mix with dough hook or by hand until all flour is incorporated. If it is still sticky, add the remaining 1/2 C. flour. Turn the dough out on a floured board and with greased hands and begin to knead dough. You must knead the dough at least 10 minutes. Place the dough in a well greased bowl. Allow it to rise until it is doubled in size, about 1-1/2 to 2 hours. Punch dough down and knead gently for a few minutes. Place dough in greased loaf or round pans. Cover with a cloth and let rise again until almost double in size. Bake at 350 degrees for 45 minutes to 1 hour or until the bread "thumps" hollow. Brushing the loaves with butter approximately 10 minutes before finishing will guarantee an even brown color.

Stilton Cheesecake

Try this cheesecake by the fire with a glass of port, sautéed walnuts, fresh pears and apples.

Crust:
1-1/2 C. bread crumbs (French bread)
1 stick melted butter
3 T. finely ground walnuts

Filling:
8 oz. Stilton cheese
1-3/4 lb. cream cheese
4 eggs
1/2 C. Half and Half
3/4 C. sour cream
1/2 tsp. salt

Combine the bread crumbs, melted butter and walnuts. Pat the mixture on the bottom of 9" springform pan and refrigerate for 30 minutes. Mix cheese together and beat in eggs, one at a time. Add remaining ingredients and mix well. Pour mixture into prepared springform pan and bake in a 325 degree oven for 1 hour. Turn the oven off and let cheesecake sit in oven for 30 minutes. Remove from oven and cool for at least two hours. Carefully remove from pan and refrigerate.

FRENCH

A Château Breakfast

Luncheon in Normandy

Le Picnique Provençal

Les Desserts au Marché

Le Diner Louis XV Style

A Château Breakfast

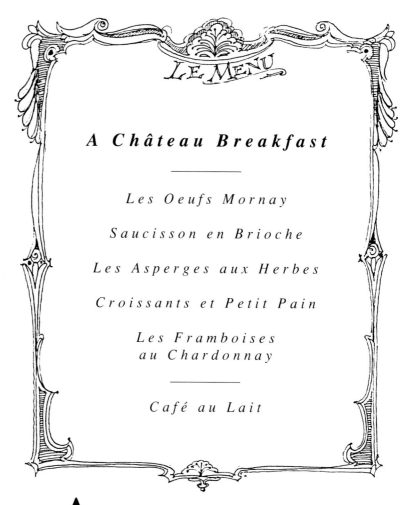

LE MENU

A Château Breakfast

Les Oeufs Mornay

Saucisson en Brioche

Les Asperges aux Herbes

Croissants et Petit Pain

*Les Framboises
au Chardonnay*

Café au Lait

Anyone with even a modest interest in interior design recognizes Country French today. Our coffee tables groan under stacks of well-written and magnificently illustrated volumes describing the unrivaled charms of Normandy, Brittany, Provence, and every other sun-drenched, cotton-printed, geranium-planted corner of Gallic paradise. For many antiquers, this is no recent romance — it is the latest chapter in a life-long love affair with France: its history, culture, architecture, food and furniture. In most books today, the magnificent works of art in wood with ormulu and gilt that epitomized the Paris salons or the courts of Fontainebleu and Versailles are slighted or ignored. It is Country French they are describ-

ing and it is Provincial furniture (1650-1880) we are discussing — that inspired carving on wood that compels us to put this country work in a charm class all by itself.

French travel folders have an urgent appeal. The chance to sample world famous cuisine from the finest, freshest home-grown ingredients and to savor world famous wines 30 feet from the vines in historic châteaux are sufficient reasons to book a seat on the next available plane. Add to that the opportunity to see the pages of the coffee table books in three dimensions and to shop for buffets and armoires in quaint backroad villages and the hunter is in heaven!

What compares to waking to a breakfast of crisp, fresh croissants and steaming café au lait, spending a day in the Loire Valley visiting a couple of châteaux to absorb the culture, the intrigue and the romance of the region, following all "antiquités" signs to their source, having an early dinner in a tiny Chenouceaux auberge of fresh local fish in a delicate buerre blanc sauce with a chilled bottle of Sancerre, followed by fresh raspberry tarts — and ending the perfect day watching a dramatic sound and light salute to Diane de Poitiers at her chateau? The only thing comparable might be indulging in a similar gluttony in Avignon or Honfleur or Le Mont St. Michel.

But, if you voyage to France to buy antiques, you will find that even paradise can have problems. Two factors contribute to the dilemma which antiquers face.

One factor is the traditional difficulty of obtaining transport for antiques in France, both within and from the country. In England, the antiques industry (and that is truly what it is) is organized to move your purchases quickly and economically from the remotest part of the island to the shipping points for consolidation. In France, as soon as you leave the environs of Paris, questions about transport are generally greeted with a roll of the eyes and a shrug of the shoulders. It is possible to hire a van — as many English and few American dealers do — and collect your goods as you buy. But if you don't do that, you can expect to have a problem consolidating goods purchased in several places for shipment in one container/crate — which is the only economical way to transport antiques.

Although most dealers in the French countryside can arrange shipping the antiques you purchase from them from their shop to your home, the French export laws often cause major delays and expense. Still, if the value of your purchase justifies the shipping expense and you're satisfied that the piece is for you, go ahead and ship...but be sure to take into account the second factor which is

and polishing...an elegant contrast to the copper. No value is lost, as the pieces could still be resilvered, and they substitute nicely for the far more expensive 19th C. copper.

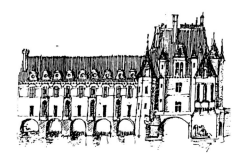

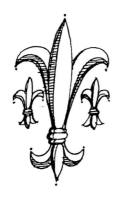

discussed below.

The increasing scarcity of the "real thing" is the second factor which makes it difficult to buy antiques in France. Those thousands of containers full of Country French antiques that have sailed for America during the last 50 years have effectively stripped most of the cottages, barns, and chicken coops of honest country tables, jelly cabinets, tole, copper and every other original antique. As availability has diminished, the price has gone up, and with the consequent temptation to over restore, to make several pieces out of parts of one and to "fake it."

Country furniture has invariably been subjected to hard use. Feet and legs were particularly vulnerable since the stone or brick floors they stood on were cleaned by sloshing buckets of water over them. The constant damp that resulted has caused many a beautifully carved snail foot to turn to sawdust. Also, most Country French furniture is made from fruitwoods that are particularly subject to woodworm. Although skillful repair or replacement of the damaged part has always been accepted as necessary to keep the piece in use, the current problem — not just in France but in England, the United States and everywhere antiques are scarce — is that the repair, replacement or other restoration on a piece is often so extensive that the item has become, in reality, a new piece instead of an antique. Moreover, with scarcity, and competition what they are today, this damaging fact may not be mentioned on the tag or pointed out to you by the dealer.

Scarcity also results in very high prices on good, original pieces. When you travel to the country of origin to buy antiques, it is reasonable to expect to find finer, earlier, more original pieces for less money than you can at home. For the most part, this is still true in England, but don't count on it in France. The only way you will succeed

in obtaining a bargain in late 20th century France is to investigate prices at home before you go so that you can tell immediately whether the price being quoted is advantageous. Learn everything you can about where and how to look for restoration and replacement — and examine everything you consider buying — upside down and inside out — under a good light.

In summary, buying antiques in France is not for the novice now, but the chance to hunt for them in Paris or the French countryside should not be missed, even if you do most of your buying in the cafés. Likewise, the chance to decorate at least part of your home with period Country French furniture and/or accessories should not be missed, even if you must buy them in England or the United States.

Hunting For A Country French Honeymoon?

A close American associate was so enchanted by "Country French" that she chose to get married in Provence — in Avignon — with parties and honeymoon in a 14th century village just across the Rhone River. Le Prieuré, an ancient stone priory converted to a tastefully luxurious hotel — in the center of romantic Villeneuve-lès-Avignon — was the site of the festivities and is, indeed, a treasure. There are fine examples of period Country French furniture with appropriate fabrics in both the public rooms and the bedrooms. The food is excellent classic/nouvelle/provincial, served in the courtyard when possible and the facilities include a library, a large pool and two tennis courts. The central location in this charming village — a jog away from one of the most interesting cities in France — in history/scenery-rich Provence completes the "Hollywood" honeymoon scene. Country French at its finest!

Les Oeufs Mornay

These eggs are a favorite breakfast or brunch recipe. They are rich and tasty. You must not make the filling until the morning you are to serve it as the mushrooms will turn the filling dark.

8 hard boiled eggs (8 because you may lose two whites when cutting them and the additional filling is nice)
6 large mushrooms
8 T. whipping cream
cayenne pepper
salt
12 artichoke bottoms (optional)

Mornay sauce:
4 T. butter
1/4 C. flour
1/2 tsp. Dijon mustard
3/4 tsp. dry mustard
cayenne pepper
1-1/2 C. milk
1 or 2 celery leaves
1 bay leaf
1/4 C. Parmesan cheese
1/4 C. Swiss cheese
1/4 — 1/2 C. Half and Half

Mince mushrooms in food processor then add egg yolks, cream, salt, and pepper. Combine until smooth. Slice eggs in half lengthwise. Fill with egg yolk and mushroom mixture. Coat bottom of au gratin pan with small amount of Mornay sauce. Place filled egg in artichoke bottom and place in au gratin pan. Top with Mornay sauce and bake at 350 degrees for 25-30 minutes or until bubbly.

Melt butter and whisk in flour and spices — let cook over medium low heat for about 5 minutes. Whisk in milk, bay leaves, celery, and let it thicken. Add cheeses and Half and Half. (Check for seasonings.)

Saucisson en Brioche

Brioche is a wonderfully tender and buttery breakfast bread. When combined with a spicy sausage or grainy Dijon mustard it makes a delicious breakfast "sandwich" — or made smaller (accompanied by a homemade chutney), a great appetizer.

Brioche dough *(combine):*
1 lb. all purpose flour
2 T. sugar
2 T. yeast
2 tsp. salt

Add:
1/2 C. milk
6 eggs
10 oz. butter at room temp.
1 egg lightly beaten

Sausage *(poach in):*
1 pint white wine
1 pint water
peppercorns
bay leaf
1 garlic clove
Dijon mustard

In a mixer combine all of the dry ingredients and then add enough milk to make a stiff dough. Add the eggs one at a time, beating well after each addition. Add butter one tablespoon at a time and beat with dough hook. Cover and let rise 1 hour or until double bulk. Punch down and roll out into a rectangular shape. Form around sausage. Place in a small buttered loaf pan seam side down. Let rise until double and brush with egg wash. Bake at 350 degrees about one hour until it "thumps" hollow.

Sausage — You can easily make your own sausage if you have a food processor, but if not, go to a specialty meat shop for a fine veal or pork sausage.

Prick sausages; poach in 1 pint white wine, 1 pint water, peppercorns, bay leaf, and 1 garlic clove for approximately 20 minutes and let cool. Coat sausage with Dijon mustard and place in the center of the dough.

Les Framboises au Chardonnay

In the countryside, fresh wild raspberries and Gatenais (honey) would be used in this recipe. The simple combination of wine and honey enhances the natural flavor of the berries.

Wash and drain raspberries carefully

Mix:
1 C. Chardonnay
1/4 tsp. fresh nutmeg
1 lb. or more honey
(Sprinkle over raspberries
   and let soak.)

Or *(a creamy fruit sauce):*
1 C. crème fraiche
2 T. Cointreau or Grand Marnier
1 tsp. grated orange zest
2 T. brown sugar
(Serve this to spoon over raspberries.)

Luncheon in Normandy

LE MENU

**Luncheon
in Normandy**

Soupe de Tomate Honfleur

Torte Sebree

*Les Hûitres
à la Hollandaise*

Les Artichauts Farcis

*Mûre à la
Mousseline de Vanille*

Pouilly Fuissé

One of the most appealing parts of traveling in Europe today is the opportunity to stay in the manor houses, châteaux, castles and even monasteries that have been converted to hotels. While some are more luxurious than others, all of these 10th-through-18th century buildings have been modernized just enough to make them acceptable to demanding international travelers without destroying the original decorative arts and architecture. Many of these landmark restorations use antique furnishings and other interior decor that are consistent with the period of the house — some of which are original and have stood in the same location for three to five hundred years. While the meals offered in such places are not necessarily

*The inspiration for the exterior architecture of this home was a farmhouse in Normandy. Apparently there was little architectural inspiration for the interior until this **1.** pair of 18th C. oak Armoire Doors were obtained by subsequent owners 60 years later. While the doors are from the North of France instead of Normandy, their elegant simplicity makes them more believable as closet doors than quaintly carved Norman ones might have been. The less permanent fixtures in this setting are some other French favorites: **2.** An oak Commode featuring fruitwood drawer fronts with original hardware, c. 1770; **3.** A superb Norman Pannetiere, c. 1750; **4.** A simple 18th C. Giltwood Mirror Frame with original 2-part glass; **5.** A luncheon service of Bretonne Faience from Quimper, c. 1985; and a few foreign rarities: **6.** An unusual Italian carved walnut Triangle Table, c. 1830, holding **7.** a Dutch Brass Footed Jardinaire with repoussé armorial design, used as a soup tureen, and **8.** a pair of Italian repoussé Brass Frames with original glass, c. 1830.*

"of the period," they are considered by guests and hosts alike to be an extremely important part of this discovery experience and tend toward gastronomic excellence, featuring the fresh local meats, fish, fruits and vegetables.

Some of our Anglophile/Francophile customers have found these entrées to an earlier age difficult to leave when vacation days end. The magnificently carved fire surrounds and overmantles and entryways have whispered secrets of a past that is too romantic to leave behind. The stone gargoyles struggling to fly off the slate roof, the bog oak lion finials that guard the stairwell and the linenfold paneling on the library walls are **history** and merit more attention than can be awarded on a short visit. The solution to this slightly over-dramatized dilemma is to bring them home...not the ones from the hotel, please...but ones similar to them that were once parts of less permanent structures. If our customers did not bring them home, they bought these wood and stone treasures from us after we did, and built them into their apartments and condos, bungalows and mansions. Now **history** is at home, adorning fireplaces, door and window frames, kitchen cabinets and garden walls. Such ingenuity does not relieve the pressure to return to the English manor or the French castle, but it does make the time between trips pass more pleasantly.

Actually, we consider these ancient-to-18th century embellishments to be far and away the best buys in today's market. They are not only the oldest of the antiques that are available in any quantity today, they are also the cheapest. The possibilities are endless: iron keys and locks, iron or brass door knockers, the doors themselves and fabulous stained glass windows, newel posts, balustrades, finials, wood or stone fire surrounds, iron fireplace fittings, parquet flooring, corbels, ceiling bosses and moldings...the list goes on and includes everything from carved walnut fragments to complete pine-paneled rooms. Equally decorative and historic are the furniture fragments...the armoire and cabinet doors, Brittany lit-clos (wall bed) panels and caryatids (the long, narrow panels that are richly carved on one side with faces and figures...romantic and grotesque — c. 1400-1800) — from defunct furniture fronts. It's exciting just pondering where these pieces came from, who made them and why, and when you think about the dramatic difference they can make in the interior and exterior of a home, it's amazing that any of them are still on the market for a paltry few hundred dollars.

One of our discoveries that may be useful to you is

17th C. French Carved Walnut Putti (angel) Panel (probably a stile panel from a 17th C. chest).

*Carved Door from Louis XV
Walnut Pannetiere, c. 1760.*

that early wood carvings…whether architectural, "furni-tural" or figural (Santos, putti, peasant figures or puppy dogs) are available all over the world at bargain prices today (that's not to say that all are bargains…German and French Gothic figures are not…but they still may be good investments). We don't generally recommend antiques as investments because they are not readily liquidated, but we think that 16th-19th century wood carvings and carved wood architectural pieces are so undervalued compared to other decorative/fine arts of similar age that they must appreciate. We hope you will benefit from this view-point…we know we do.

Much of the finest carving on French furniture has been done in Normandy…particularly on the wedding armoires for which the region is famous. We're always shocked when a customer looks at all those marvelously imaginative love birds and floral bouquets with disdain and declares intent to find something "a little simpler." What could be more simple than this expression of love? Normandy is famous also for butter, eggs and Calvados. While some people deride Le Mont St. Michel as a "tourist trap," it is still our favorite Norman destination with the fabled omelette at La Mere Poulard our goal for luncheon…followed by just a drop of the native apple brandy…to sustain the treasure hunt, of course.

Soupe de Tomate Honfleur

This is one of Le Picnique's most "asked for" soups. It has loads of flavor and is good hot in the winter and cold in the summer. It can be made chunky or smooth enough to sip.

1/4 C. butter
1/4 C. olive oil
2 onions, coarsely chopped
4 stacks celery, coarsely
    chopped
4 carrots, coarsely chopped
4 cloves of garlic, minced
1/2 C. parsley
1/4 C. balsamic vinegar
salt & generous amount of
    cracked pepper
1 C. fresh basil, minced
2 T. dried basil

Add:
12-14 whole tomatoes, skinned
    (or add 3 cans
    whole tomatoes)
1 15-oz. can tomato paste
4 C. whipping cream

Sauté first 11 ingredients together until fork tender. Add tomatoes and tomato paste. Cook over medium to low heat for one hour. Let cool and purée in food processor. Add as much cream as you like. Adjust seasoning. You may serve this soup cold or hot with fresh basil leaves as garnish.

Torte Sebree

This torte is full of the robust flavors of the Normandy countryside. Everything can be prepared the night before and then quickly layered the next day and baked.

1 pkg. puff pastry or
    1 lb. fresh puff pastry
1 lb. spinach (sauté in small
    amount of butter and
    squeeze dry)
1/4 C. each fresh sorrel and
    fresh basil, coarsely chopped
1 clove garlic

In 9" greased springform pan, cut 2 rounds of puff pastry to fit top and bottom of torte. Cut rectangular pieces to fit around side. (You can purchase puff pastry from a local patisserie.) Put bottom round in first and then collar around inside. Press sides and bottom together to form a seal. Layer spinach mixture (spinach, sorrel, basil and garlic), ham, pepper, onion, tomato,

4 C. country ham or smoked
   chicken, sliced
1 red pepper sliced
1 green pepper, sliced
1/2 red onion, sliced
6 tomatoes sliced and drained
5 eggs beaten
salt & pepper
1 lb. sliced mushrooms
   (sautéed until almost dry)
4 C. grated Cheddar cheese
2 C. Swiss cheese

mushroom and cheese. Beat the eggs and pour over the top. Place top pastry on the filling. Pinch the edges together to form a seal. Decorate the top with pastry braids or leaves. Then brush with eggwash (1 egg, 1 tablespoon water). Bake 90 minutes at 375 degrees. Let rest 30 minutes before serving. Release sides and cut like a cake.

Les Hûitres à la Hollandaise

Oysters that cling to the Brittany coast are shipped all over France and are delicious served barely poached with sorrell or a red pepper Hollandaise.

24 oysters in shell

Flaked crab meat
Sorrell
1/2 tsp. minced red pepper

Hollandaise (in a metal
   bowl whisk):
3 egg yolks
4 T. water
2 tsp. lemon juice
pinch cayenne pepper
pinch pepper
pinch fresh nutmeg
1/2 tsp. salt
2 sticks butter, clarified
2 red peppers
2 green peppers

Shuck oysters, reserve shells and poach oysters gently in 2 C. white wine and 2 C. water, 2 shallots (minced), salt and pepper, and lemon juice until edges curl.

Whip yolks, water, juice — seasoning over hot, but not boiling water until thick and creamy. Whip in butter (about) 1 tablespoon at a time until very thick and creamy. Char red and green peppers over open flame. Put the peppers in paper bag and let steam until skin is easily removed. Peel off skin — mince and drain on paper towels. Sprinkle empty oyster shells with flaked crab meat, pinch of sorrell and 1/2 teaspoon minced pepper. Top with oyster. Cover with Hollandaise and place under broiler. Quickly brown tops and serve immediately. Add remaining minced peppers right before serving.

Les Artichauts Farcis

This is a beautiful and delicate presentation that, with the addition of fresh fruit, would make for a wonderful lunch.

6 artichokes, trimmed
1 lemon
1 bay leaf
1 tsp. whole peppercorns
1 tsp. olive oil
Salt
Parmesan cheese

Cook artichokes in water with lemon, bay leaf, salt, olive oil, and peppercorn until heart is fork tender. Place in ice water to cool and retard cooking. After cooling, remove choke and rinse thoroughly. Turn upside down and let drain. Dust inside of the artichoke with Parmesan cheese.

Asparagus Soufflé:
1/4 C. unsalted butter
1/4 C. flour
1 C. whole milk
1/2 tsp. salt
Pinch cayenne pepper
1/2 tsp. dry mustard
4 oz. shredded Gruyere cheese
*1 lb. fresh asparagus, steamed
    until tender and finely
    chopped*
4 eggs, separated

Melt butter in a heavy saucepan over low heat and whisk in flour. Let cook for approximately 2 minutes. Gradually add milk and whisk until mixture is thick and bubbly. Add spices and cheese. Stir until cheese is melted. Add asparagus.

Beat 4 egg yolks until thick. Whisk 1/4 C. asparagus mixture into egg yolks then blend with remaining asparagus mixture. Stir well. Beat 4 egg whites until stiff but not dry and gently fold into asparagus mixture.

Spoon soufflé into prepared artichokes (approximately half full). Bake at 350 degrees for 30-40 minutes or until soufflé is completely set. Serve immediately.

Mûre à la Mousseline de Vanille

This rich and creamy sauce spooned over berries and served with a crisp sparkling wine is a delicious dessert.

1 vanilla bean, split
3/4 C. heavy whipping cream
1 whole egg
2 egg yolks
1/2 C. sugar
Pinch of salt
1-1/2 T. Kirsch
1 C. vanilla yogurt

Place vanilla bean into cream. Cover and refrigerate overnight. In a double boiler whisk eggs, egg yolk, sugar and salt together and place over simmering water until the mixture is thick. Remove mixture and place in a bowl. Stir in Kirsch. Let cool and whisk yogurt into egg mixture. Remove vanilla bean from the cream. Whip cream until soft peaks form. Fold the cream into the yogurt mixture and refrigerate.

Le Picnique Provençal

LE MENU

Le Picnique
Provençal

———

Le Potage Lapin

Tarte aux Tomates

Salade de Thon

*Suprème aux Canard
Fumé aux Poires*

Fromage Indien

———

Dom Perignon

We all understand that just because an item ages does not mean it becomes an antique. Most current inventory of gift and souvenir shops around the world is mass-produced by machines and, unless the rules miraculously change, will never, never be antiques. They could, however, become valuable as "collectibles" if that whimsy of fashion continues on course…in 20 years or less. For example, the perishable plastic toys that were all over the floor before we heard about oil shortages will undoubtedly become valuable "collectibles" — just as the toys of the '20s and '30s have become. There are few of us from that generation who have not gently chastised our mothers for giving away the lead soldiers and "Mickey Mouse" figures.

Ethnic Doll in Regional Dress of Brittany — made 19th C. to present.

Likewise, there are some of today's handicrafts that will stand the more rigorous tests of time, increase in value as we use and enjoy them and become antiques…in 100 years or so…maybe just in time for our grandchildren to appreciate our wise and prophetic purchases. Our favorite antique candidates are holiday decorations and ornaments, particularly the one-of-a-kind Santa Claus/ Father Christmas figures that make an annual appearance on gift shop — and antique store — shelves. Actually, it's the more somber, Renaissance-style Father Christmas or Pere Noel figures that appeal to us…partly because they have an antique look no matter how new they are and partly because they seem to represent more effectively the real spirit of the season than the laughing department-store-style Santas. Many of our customers start holiday ornament collections for their children and children of friends. Most of these adorable creations are handmade or at least hand painted and represent, we think, at the current $2 -$12 price range, the most meaningful gift for the money one could give…to a child or adult…without considering their extra value as pre-antiques.

Consider also, if you will, the current crop of baskets — handmade from natural materials in third world nations — each one, in construction, slightly different from all the rest. Each basket, in design and materials, represents a certain time and culture. They are extremely cheap and plentiful. Don't you think that the ones from 1980-90 that are still around in 2050 will be treasures?

International dolls — often totally handcrafted — are an enigma. The only ones that seem to have achieved any collector status are the French ones…notably those from Quimper. Will other ethnic dolls catch on some day and will you have some when they do? When it costs so little to second-guess the market, we can all have a

Father Christmas has come prepared! In addition to old snowshoes **1.** and wooden skis **2.**, he has brought a feast into the forest — a Country French picnique, if you please — a princely repast replete with his bag of fresh game and fish to be cooked over the open fire! He has also wisely included a back-up banquet from Keitha's kitchen in case the snow puts out the fire, with baguettes and bottles of Dom Perignon, all neatly tucked away on **3.** a Turkish Prayer Rug in **4.** a delightful Provincial Children's Sleigh. Should some antique hunters happen by, he has plenty to share.
(See page 85.)

go at it.

Another good bet for the future as evidenced by past performance is faience — the charm-filled French tin-glazed pottery — particularly that from Quimper in Brittany. When a chipped saucer from a 1930s luncheon set is already selling for 10-15 times the original cost, the trend looks good. The provincial handpainting on Quimper as well as on Rouen and Gien pottery makes each piece unique, even though current production is sufficient to provide complete luncheon and dinner services for brides and other astute collectors in several different patterns. Quimper is clearly a market phenomenon in that its great Country French appeal has apparently allowed it to skip the time requirements for antiques. It is the rare flea mar-

Faience plate similar to that made in Quimper, Brittany.

ket or house sale that does not offer some and, although the value is widely recognized, bargains are plentiful in the more common pieces. Unusual shapes from the early 1900s are already bringing big prices and worth focusing on when you're treasure cruising the next flea market. If you get serious about collecting faience, the output from 18th century France has so much to offer in the way of unsophisticated provincial excellence that the high prices now should not dissuade you — they surely will not seem high five years from now.

Contemplation of such significant investment possibilities would be aided by a crystal ball, but definitely requires a clear head. We recommend a winter picnic in the woods…preferably snowy woods. The choice of food could depend on the country the woods are in — and your game hunting expertise — or you could have it prepared for you at Le Picnique. But the beverage must be champagne — to toast your future as a treasure anticipator. We've mentioned a few potentials, but there are many others out there…just waiting for you!

Suprème aux Canard–Fumé aux Poires

Smoking duck is quite easy and produces a very moist and flavorful breast. Chutney is a fresh, tart way of enhancing the smoked flavor.

5-6 lb. duck, breasts removed, wash and pat dry

Marinate breasts overnight in:
1 C. soy sauce
2 shallots
2 garlic
1/4 lb. sugar
1/2 tsp. ground ginger or
*   1 tsp. fresh ginger, minced*

Pear Chutney
Simple Syrup:
1 C. sugar
1 C. water

4 pears, coarsely chopped
2 grated onions
1/2 green and 1/2 red pepper, coarsely chopped

Spices:
Mix equal amounts of the following spices and add 1 T. of the mixture to Simple Syrup mixture.
cardamon
nutmeg
garlic cloves
cinnamon
zest enough lemon, orange and lime to make 1 T. and add to above

Take breast out of marinade and place duck over medium coals sprinkled with hickory chips (which have soaked in water for 30 minutes). Put lid on tightly and let smoke, rotating every 15 minutes for approximately 2 hours or until coals have died (should be a mahogany color).

Note: If duck is not done, place in oven at 350 degrees for 15 minutes (cover tightly).

Simple Syrup — Boil 1 C. sugar and 1 C. water in small saucepan together until syrup consistency. Remove from heat and stir in remaining ingredients. Let steep for an hour.

Salade de Thon

Fresh tuna that is caught off the Atlantic Coast is sold at fish auctions to Parisians, East Coast chefs, housewives and fish mongers, or flown to Kansas City that afternoon. It is delicious grilled, baked or raw with soy sauce and fresh ginger.

1-1/2 lb. fresh tuna
salt & pepper
1 red pepper, coarsely
  chopped
1 green pepper, coarsely
  chopped
2 green onions, coarsely
  chopped
2 stalks celery, coarsely
  chopped

Rub tuna with olive oil and grill over medium coals — about 10 minutes per side. Chunk with fork and very gently fold peppers, onion, celery and tuna together while adding the vinaigrette.

Vinaigrette — Mix together: 1/2 C. balsamic vinegar, 1-1/2 C. olive oil, 1 clove garlic, 1 teaspoon Dijon mustard, 1/2 C. minced arugula leaves, salt & pepper, fresh basil to taste and 1 teaspoon capers.

Tarte aux Tomates

This tomato tart, made from fresh farm tomatoes and basil is a provincial delight. It tastes wonderful the next day as an hors d' oeuvre.

4 large ripe and firm tomatoes
  sliced and salted, left to
  drain on paper towels
1 lb. Gruyere cheese grated
1 C. slivered smoked bacon
2 T. Dijon mustard
2 T. grated Parmesan cheese
fresh basil and tarragon
  to taste with minced
  garlic cloves
freshly ground pepper
melted butter

Prepare short crust pastry as in the Welsh Treacle Torte (see index) eliminating the lemon peel and vanilla. Line with wax paper and fill with beans to prevent shrinkage and bake at 400 degrees for 10 minutes. Let cool. Coat bottom of pastry with mustard then layer cheese, bacon and tomatoes in crust. Sprinkle with fresh herbs and drizzle with butter, ground pepper and sprinkle Parmesan on top. Bake at 375 degrees for 20-25 minutes or until it has browned.

Potage Lapin

Potage Lapin is a cherished family recipe in France. It should be served with either homemade noodles or baby potatoes. Chicken may be substituted for the rabbit but it does not produce the same provincial flavors.

*1 Rabbit, skinned and cut into
    serving pieces
2 — 4 T. flour
salt & pepper
3 garlic cloves
2 stalks celery
2 large onions, diced
2 carrots, minced
1 C. smoked bacon, diced
1 bottle Merlot
Bay Leaves
Thyme
Basil*

Marinate rabbit for 24 hours in wine, 1 clove garlic, 1 onion and herbs. Drain and reserve this liquid. Dry rabbit pieces with a paper towel and then dredge them in flour that has been seasoned with salt and pepper. Sauté bacon until crisp and add rabbit to pan. Brown on all sides. Remove the rabbit to a casserole dish. Sauté 1 onion, 2 stalks celery, 2 minced carrots and garlic in the same pan. Pour over rabbit. Add marinade and enough chicken stock to cover. Bring to a boil, then cover tightly. Place rabbit in oven at 325 degrees for approximately 2 hours. Check seasonings and at this time you may want to add a little cognac or additional herbs.

Fromage Indien

Brie is a versatile and delicious cheese. Wrapping it in puff pastry creates a beautiful display that we use for both desserts and appetizers.

*1 lb. fresh Brie
1 lb. fresh puff pastry
1 jar of Homemade Cranberry
    or Apple Chutney
Egg wash (1 egg, 1 T. water)*

Spray 10" pie pan with vegetable oil. Place Brie on top of puff pastry round cut 1" larger than cheese. Top cheese with preferred chutney. Cut larger round of pastry and design the top of pastry so that chutney can be seen either through lattice-work or cut outs. Seal edges and coat with egg wash. Bake at 375 degrees until golden brown. Let cool slightly.

Note: If using an herbed brie, try topping it with grilled red pepper, onion, and eggplant for a wonderful appetizer.

Les Desserts au Marché

LE MENU

Les Desserts au Marché

Gateau au Chocolat

Tarte au Citron

Croquembouche

Gateau au Ruban de Chocolat

Crème Caramel

Tarte d' Automne

Tarte aux Fraises

Truffes

Every street in Paris has a pretty pastry shop, each offering a dozen delicacies worth the calories — many of which we have tried. But rewarding as those spots are, our favorite pastry source has long been an unpretentious café on Rue Paul Bert in the middle of Le Marché aux Puces — the world-famous Paris flea market. (Actually, the last time we ate there, the quality of the tarts had diminished considerably but we will return just in case the real chef was off that day.)

For reasons given previously, we have not shipped from France recently, but that does not preclude our going there and enjoying looking for treasures in "old favorite" places. Our first stops are always in the area near our

The *1. Louis XV Fruitwood Buffet, c. 1770, speaks volumes about why the Country French style is so popular with its graceful curves and charming carving, and even more about why Country French antiques are far more desirable than the modern reproductions — **nothing** but centuries of waxing and rubbing by hand can give this warm, mellow finish to a piece of cherry wood. Other accoutrements are: 2. Numerous small 19th C. French Copper Saucepans and Jelly Molds; 3. Three old French Bread Baskets; 4. A copper and brass Plateau, c. 1920 from a Paris pastry shop (probably originally silver-plated) and a 5. repoussé brass Genre Plaque, c. 1840 and a great selection of glamorous desserts by the chefs of Le Picnique.*

preferred Left-Bank hotel. The neighborhood of Rue de l' Université near Rue des St. Peres sparkles with gorgeous galleries of decorative and fine arts including one that specializes in paintings, wood carvings, bronzes and all kinds of paraphenalia that have to do with "le chasse." Just window shopping here is sufficient to properly stimulate the treasure hunting instincts.

Over near the Louvre is the prestigious Louvre des Antiquaires with several floors of elegant shops specializing in "high end" merchandise — generally rare pieces at rarified prices — but it is possible to buy there and spend a day there — looking and learning. One tiny shop sells only early military medals of great variety and beauty — an interesting way to learn military history while building

a unique collection.

We have admitted partiality to the London markets but we must agree that no antique market we have been to or heard of rivals Le Marché aux Puces in St. Ouen on the northern rim of Paris. It is not only the largest antique furniture market in the world, it is also the most confusing. It was our third Paris buying trip before we discovered that Vernaison, the only market where we had been buying, was just one of five major markets-within-the-market. We know tourists and even dealers who have become lost in the mass of peripheral stalls that sell blue jeans, leather jackets and the latest rock tapes and never reached the flea market at all!

Louis XVI Fauteuil (open arm chair), c. 1790.

Take the Metro to Porte de Clingancourt and then walk three blocks north, or perhaps a cab is a better choice (but 20 times as expensive) to insure that you get to the right place. Wear comfortable shoes and clothes, and if you are a potential buyer, avoid looking too touristy or too prosperous. (A good rule for every antique market.)

The market is open weekly on Saturday, Sunday and Monday only. There is no need to miss croissants at the hotel as nothing much is open before 10 a.m. The unusual feature of this market is that each dealer has his own shop — not just a stall — in some cases under large roofed areas, in others along either side of an open walkway. On Saturday, there are temporary street stalls offering a wild variety of mostly-new-some-old smalls. For various reasons — mostly having to do with price — we were never able to buy good small accessories at Marché aux Puces. This is basically a market of furniture, most of which is 19th and 20th century. There are some 18th century treasures with 21st century prices, however, and enough late 18th and early 19th century Country French furniture, architectural pieces and garden accessories at

The principal markets within *Le Marché aux Puces* generalize or specialize as follows (in order of appearance down the Rue de Rosiers):

Vernaison — we thought this was all there was — and could buy a container full of Country French here twenty years ago — but no more. It is still an interesting market with alleys in every direction and stalls featuring early fabrics, tassels, toys, dolls, children's clothes, and posters, plus French, English and Oriental furniture — period to today. There is a café in the back with live music on market days.

Biron — the best furniture stop featuring a good selection of 18th and 19th century English and French, formal and country, as well as hard-to-find accessories. There is even a reliable shipper at the far end.

Cambo — a magnificent variety of paintings, arms and armour, silver, jewelry, lead soldiers, garden accessories and several periods of furniture.

Serpette — a small market with elegant antique linens, gilt-bronzes, arms and Napoleonica, tapestries, Deco and Nouveau furniture and accessories.

Paul Bert — our favorite with the café of the same name on the corner has open passageways between a labyrinth of covered shops featuring architectural pieces, armoire doors, fire surrounds, garden sculpture, urns and lots of country furniture. This market and Vernaison are less elegant and expensive than the others.

In the front corner of Vernaison you can buy a detailed guide to the market that describes certain shops and restaurants with entertainment.

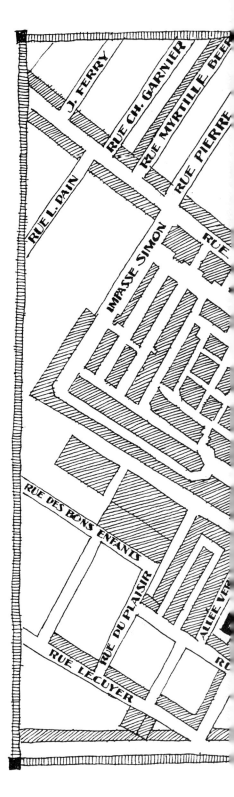

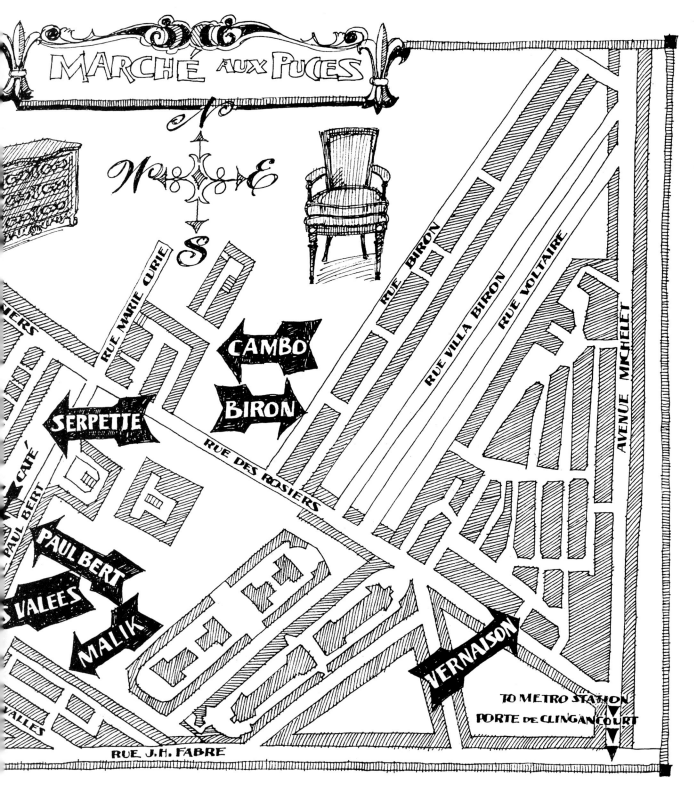

TREASURES

Le Marché aux Puces — Paris *(North)*

Every Saturday, Sunday and Monday. 10 a.m. to 5 p.m. (approximately)
Rue de Rosiers in St. Ouen at Porte de Clingancourt

negotiable prices to make this Paris flea market the number one treasure hunter's target in France.

There is more bargaining going on here than in England, but the spontaneity is hampered significantly if you must deal in two languages. Writing the numbers may result in a negotiated price, but the problem remains that it is too easy...sometimes even convenient...for the dealer to misunderstand your questions about the age, restoration and provenance of a piece. Be sure you know what you are buying. If you expect to buy important pieces, you may want to hire an antiques commissionnaire to accompany you in order to translate the deal, handle the papers and arrange shipping.

Most of the flea market dealers have shops elsewhere in France and bring in fresh merchandise weekly. If you're spending at least two weekends in Paris, and don't see what you want on your first visit, try the next week. The smalls you find can be shipped in your suitcase. Larger pieces can be handled by one of several shippers located right in the markets. The dealer will probably suggest a favorite...advice you may want to take...but check around first.

Plan your day at the flea market around a stop for lunch at one of the many popular sidewalk cafés (we still prefer Paul Bert, even though the cuisine is not haut). Sitting down at an old marble-topped Parisian café table does wonders for the tired legs, strained eyes and frayed nerves of a flea market hunter. There is so much going on in so many languages which you can now observe and enjoy with a large carafe of house wine, a hearty provincial-style lunch and, perhaps, a piece of the once-world's-best-tarte-aux-fraises (ask the waiter to save one of these treasures for you when you order lunch).

Bon Appetit!

Gateau au Chocolat

This is our favorite gateau and one that people come back to eat time and time again. It is like a giant truffle. It may be filled with fresh raspberries and strawberries and topped with whipped cream.

2 sticks butter
4 oz. semi-sweet
chocolate chips
1 C. sugar
1/2 C. espresso coffee
1 tsp. vanilla
4 eggs

Melt sugar, chocolate and butter together, stir in coffee and vanilla. Let cool. Stir in beaten eggs. Bake at 350 degrees for 40 minutes. The middle will not appear to be done, but it will set up overnight in the refrigerator.

Frost with whipped cream that has been sweetened with powdered sugar, flavored with vanilla. Sprinkle whipped cream with toasted slivered almonds.

Tarte au Citron

Use short crust recipe for the Welsh Treacle Torte (see index). Fill tart shell with waxed paper and beans to weigh down the pastry and bake 20 minutes at 375 degrees or until brown. Fill with lemon curd and top with fresh blueberries for variety.

Lemon Curd:
8 T. butter
1-1/2 C. sugar
1/2 C. fresh lemon juice
2 tsp. lemon zest
1 tsp. fresh lime juice
1 tsp. lime zest
5 eggs beaten

Melt butter in saucepan, add sugar, lemon and lime juice and zest. Cook about 5 minutes or until sugar dissolves. Add eggs slowly and continue cooking until thick. Cover top with plastic wrap and refrigerate. This curd will keep for two weeks in the refrigerator. The addition of lime makes this tart very tart! It is one of the most requested desserts in Le Picnique.

Croquembouche

Although this dessert takes some last minute preparation, it is a spectacular holiday presentation. The crème patisserie can be flavored with rum, or Grand Marnier or a little Framboise.

Pâté Choux:
1-1/2 sticks butter
2 C. water
2 T. sugar
1-1/2 C. flour
6 large eggs

Melt butter in the water and sugar over low heat. Remove the mixture from the heat and beat in the flour with a wooden spoon. Place the mixture back on the heat and stir 2-3 minutes. This will form a mass and a film on the bottom of the pan. Remove from heat and add eggs one at a time, beating vigorously after each egg. With a large pastry tube, form puffs on a buttered baking sheet. With feather, glaze the top of each puff with egg and water smoothing the tops as you go. Put in oven at 425 degrees for 20 minutes and remove from oven. Pierce each puff with a knife to allow steam to escape. Return the puffs to the oven for 10 minutes. Cool puffs. (They may be frozen at this stage.)

Crème Patisserie:
2 C. milk, scalded with
    1/4 C. ground hazelnuts
1/2 C. sugar
6 egg yolks
6 generous T. sugar
1/2 C. flour
2 T. butter
vanilla
2 T. Meyers rum

Beat 6 egg yolks and gradually add sugar, continuing to beat until thick and pale. Mix in the flour and add scalded milk in dribbles. Put this mixture into a medium size heavy saucepan and stir constantly over medium high heat. Stir vigorously until mixture becomes thick and smooth. Add the butter, vanilla, and rum. Let this mixture cool with plastic wrap on top to prevent crust from forming.

Caramel:
2 C. sugar
3/4 C. water
3 T. corn syrup

Bring these three ingredients to a boil over high heat. Cover the pan for a minute and then uncover it. Boil the syrup until it becomes an amber color. Keep caramel over very low heat while preparing the croquembouche.

Fill the cream puffs with crème patisserie and place the puffs in a circle of the desired diameter on dessert plate. Drizzle syrup around and between puffs. The caramel will hold the puff together. Add layer on layer to form a cone shape of filled puffs, continuing to drizzle or dip each puff into syrup. After that is completed, let syrup start to cool as you make circles around dessert with spoon — drizzling and spinning sugar all over puffs.

Tarte d'Automne

Pastries are not offered after most meals in France but a slice of this tart in the afternoon with a glass of sauterne or cup of espresso is wonderfully satisfying.

Crust:
1/2 C. butter, room temp.
1/3 C. sugar
1 tsp. vanilla
3/4 C. flour
1/2 C. ground almonds

Cream the butter, sugar, vanilla and blend in nuts and flour. Spread dough on inside of an 8" springform pan.

Filling:
16 oz. cream cheese
3/4 C. sugar
2 eggs
1/2 tsp. vanilla
grated zest of 1 lemon
1/2 tsp. grated fresh nutmeg

Beat the filling ingredients together. Toss apple and pear slices with cinnamon sugar. Pour 1/2 cheese mixture in crust and then place apples and pear in concentric circles in center of tarte. Top with remaining cheese and bake at 450 degrees for 10 minutes and 400 degrees for 25 minutes. Remove from pan and drizzle caramel decoratively on top. (Refer to Crème Caramel recipe — see index.)

Le Diner Louis XV Style

LE MENU

Le Diner
Louis XV Style

Saucisson aux
Fruits de Mer

Puligny Montrachet

Fenouil avec le Jambon

Pommes de Terre
aux Herbes

Carré d'Agneau
Gallerie

Cos d'Estournel St. Emilion

Crème Caramel avec
Poires Sautées

Château d'Yquem

When new reproduction furniture comes on the market at extremely high prices, it would be logical to assume that the original period pieces from which the new furniture was copied are no longer available. In the case of Country French furniture, such an assumption, however logical it might seem, is simply not valid. The new "designer" armoires, buffets and farm tables are in the department stores today at hefty prices, but fortunately for the antique collector, there are still many originals for sale, and quite a few have lower price tags. Choosing old Country French over a new reproduction is an easy decision for most of us to make, but the opportunity cannot last, so get moving! Let's take a look at what you can find

and where.

Period French homes — cottage or château — had to have armoires because they had no closets. These large double-door wardrobes provided the essential storage in every room and were the primary decoration. City dwellers had more sophisticated versions, but the typical armoire is Country French in concept…raised on short straight or cabriole legs (the latter customarily have curled or "snail" feet) and topped with a separate cornice. The Parisian and northern France versions are quite plain while the Normandy and Brittany armoires feature the carved hearts, birds and flowers that are the essence of "Country French."

Louis XV Normandy Armoire, c. 1770.

In U.S. homes today, one well-placed antique armoire can provide more provincial character (and storage) than any other piece of furniture. You should be able to find a choice of 18th and early 19th century armoires in every major U.S. city, in woods and styles to suit your taste and in sizes to fit specific storage requirements for a TV/entertainment center, bar or even refrigerator. In some cases, the separate armoire doors from period pieces that are no longer in one piece are just as effective and less costly. We've had many customers build these in as closet or bookcase doors for no more money than a good new pair of doors would cost. It is important to note that armoires are made in sections held together by pegs which can be taken apart for moving up narrow stairs or in small elevators.

Early buffets abound also; some with two drawers over two doors and some with just two doors: either provides excellent storage for china, crystal and silver in the dining room or a TV in the living room. Styles follow those of armoires. 19th century buffets are fairly common and reasonable. As with armoires, 18th century buffets are

For our French finale, we are pleased to present 200 years of country furniture, c. 1720-1920.

1. The period Louis XV carved wood frame is resting on 2. an 18th C. Spanish Colonial (Mexican!) Altar and holding 3. an 18th C. carved wood Santo of similar background. 4. The Louis XV-style Refectory Table, c. 1860, with 2-color parquet top, unusual "X" stretcher and hairy paw feet is a superior and older-than-usual example of this extra-convenient table style with self-storing leaves. 5. The set of eight cane-seat chairs are Louis XV-style also, c. 1880, and happen to have "X" stretchers although they do not match this table, nor would we want them if they did. (See text for rationale.) The centerpiece is the Country French version of the finale show-stopper — 6. an 18th C. carved wood basket with a lid of carved wood game (rabbits, pheasant, quail and duck); 7. this rare set of Bretonne Quimper was probably made for a hotel or Inn, c. 1920; 8. an 18th C. giltwood Barometer — most don't function any more, but

more scarce and expensive. One word of caution: we have been in workshops in both England and France that were "restoring" French buffets by taking a pair of nice old doors and attaching them to a brand new carcass, made in the time-honored ways with new lumber and a few old boards. You can tell these newborns quite easily as the makers seldom bother to hand-adze back boards or smooth off the interior rough edges or hide the new stain, but you must use your eyes and fingers to examine before you buy. (Even this sort of piece is preferred to an entirely new one if the price is right.)

Farmhouse tables constitute another category of available originals. Rectangular bases with square, tapered legs supporting plank tops are the norm. Invariably, the legs of these tables are too short and/or the aprons (the horizontal board just under and at right angles to the top) are too deep to accommodate American knees comfortably. Raised feet (3"-5" blocks are attached and blended into the legs) and/or "shaped" aprons (C-shaped or scalloped sections are cut from the apron) are the common changes made to allow legs under the table. Both modifications may be essential for use as a dining table and, therefore, acceptable. The legs on small farm tables are often cut down to coffee table height or built up to writing table height. These alterations can increase the desirability and therefore, the value of farm tables, thus constituting an exception to the general rule that alterations of antiques reduce value.

Some farm tables (or copies thereof) have a long, self-storing leaf in each end that will pull out to almost double the length of the table. These "refectory" tables are based on the 16th -17th century removable top monastery tables and offer great flexibility in the dining room. 18th and 19th century refectories command a much higher price than the fixed top farm tables, even more if they have cabriole legs. Knowing that those farmhouse tables (both the plain ones and the refectories) which have cabriole legs are in greater demand than those which have straight ones has prompted some restorers or dealers to remove the straight legs and replace them with cabrioles. The shop price may be raised $1,000 without any acknowledgement of this radical replacement. However, it's hard to get a perfect color match or disguise the recent work in attaching the legs to the top, so you can probably detect such substitutions.

The more common and even more popular refectory tables are shorter and wider with parquet tops and cabriole legs. The earliest ones we have had were made around c. 1840, with most at c. 1890-1930. The later ones were copies of the earlier and commonly parts of many-piece sets including a large buffet, a small buffet à deux corps with glazed top to display china, a refectory table

*the decorative value is worth the price; **9**. a provincial cast-iron Chandelier to provide non-electric candlelight for romantic French dinners; **10**. a Normandy pine "wedding" Buffet à Deux Corps, c. 1800; and barely visible back in the corner, a French Country requirement...**11**. Copper Lavabo on Stand, c. 1820, all seen against the appropriate background of vivid reds and blues in this **12**. Turkish Oushak carpet, c. 1935.*

Louis XV Corner Chair having carved back and cabriole legs, c. 1770.

and six to ten chairs. The sets have been deliberately split up because the individual pieces will sell for much more that way (a matched set of furniture is an anathema to designers for style reasons, and to collectors for age reasons). While they were mass-produced with handcrafting limited to the carving, the versatility of these tables and their Country French appeal have made them very popular. The chairs are also in demand because they are sturdy and they look like antiques. Since period dining tables and chairs are almost impossible to find and incredibly expensive, these Louis XV-style refectories and rush seat chairs, have become a reasonable alternative which continue to increase in value just like the antiques.

There are many other period Country French possibilities: Vaisseliers (French version of a Welsh dresser), Bibliothèques (shallow armoires for books with glazed or wire-front doors), Bonnetieres (single door armoires, originally for hats), Commodes (large chests of drawers — one of the great French contributions to the art of furniture making), Tallcase Clocks, Petrins and Pannetieres (rare dough boxes on stands with spindle frame bread coolers to hang on wall above) and the classic cast iron Butchers' Tables and Bakers' Racks — with dates from 1750-60 to 1830-40.

Where are they? Certainly there are fine pieces available in France that can be brought to the United States (with some difficulties, as previously mentioned). Many English dealers make bi-weekly treks across the French countryside, gathering goodies into their vans from remote barns to bring to England. We find that we can buy and ship French furniture more economically from England than from France.

Perhaps an even better source is the United States. So much of the best French furniture is already here and

changing households keep it circulating. Good pieces often sell quite reasonably — even at New York auctions — and they frequently show up in provincial estate sales and shops. But with the current popularity of Country French, the supply of good items, reasonably priced, cannot last. So, venture forth and buy today. You and your children and your grandchildren will be glad you did.

Louis XV Commode having serpentine front and snail feet, c. 1760.

Saucisson aux Fruits de Mer

These "boudins" are very special — light and yet very rich. They can be made the day before and the filling can also be used to make turbon of sole. (Simply butter a ramekin — line with filet of sole and fill center with filling. Bake at 350 degrees for 20-30 minutes. Serve with herbed beurre blanc.)

1 lb. white fish
3 egg whites
1-1/2 C. whipping cream
1/4 lb. bay scallops, chopped
1/2 lb. shrimp, coarsely
*   chopped*
6 oz. salmon, coarsely chopped
1 T. fresh lemon juice
2 T. dried tarragon, or
*   4 tlb. fresh*
2 tsp. salt
1/8 tsp. fresh nutmeg
1/4 tsp. cayenne pepper
1 pkg. phyllo pastry

Tarragon butter:
clarify 2 C. butter
2 T. fresh tarragon
pinch cayenne and
*   nutmeg*
clove of minced
*   garlic*
1 lb. shallots,
*   minced*
juice from 1 lemon

In cold processor bowl grind white fish and with machine running pour egg whites through the feed tube and process until smooth. Place in a bowl over ice water. Fold cream a little at a time until it is incorporated. Stir in remaining ingredients. Place 1/2 C. mixture onto 6" plastic wrap rectangle. Roll up and twist ends in opposite direction to form "sausage". Place this sausage in 6" foil wrap and twist ends again. Gently poach sausage in water for 30-40 minutes. Take out and drain excess water. Let cool.

Melt 1 C. butter. Place 3 layers of phyllo pastry buttering each layer thoroughly. Wrap each sausage in the pastry. Tuck ends under and butter top. Place in 400 degree oven until pastry is brown — 15 minutes. Serve sausage with a tarragon butter.

Carré d'Agneau Gallerie

Although this recipe is quite rich, it is also delicious with a Madeira or a wine reduction sauce. The pâté recipe (omit 3 slices bread) is delicious baked and then wrapped in puff pastry as an appetizer.

3 — 3-1/2 lb. loin of lamb
salt & pepper
3 slivered garlic cloves
fresh rosemary
2 T. butter
fresh thyme

Butterfly loin and pound to flatten piece evenly. Layer fresh spinach leaves all over meat and then add 1/2" layer of pâté on top of this. Roll meat and tie securely every 2". Quickly sauté the loin in 2 tablespoons butter, 1 teaspoon fresh rosemary and thyme, salt and freshly ground pepper and 2 tablespoons olive oil about 2-3 minutes per side. Bake in 400 degree oven for 20-30 minutes. (Check after 20 minutes to see if it needs to continue to bake. Remember that meat does continue to cook after it is removed from the oven.)

Pâté:

2 medium onions
3 cloves garlic
6 oz. salt pork
2 T. chicken livers
5 eggs
8 slices firm white bread
    with crusts removed
2 tsp. freshly ground pepper
1 tsp. salt
2 T. mixed thyme, oregano,
    rosemary

Place onions and garlic into processor bowl and chop finely. Add cubed salt pork (rinsed), chicken liver, eggs, bread and remaining ingredients. Process until rather smooth. The onions should be left somewhat chunky.

Crème Caramel

Crème Caramel is our favorite dessert and this recipe always produces a smooth version. These are good placed on crisp tuiles and topped with fresh raspberries.

Caramel *(boil):*
3/4 C. sugar
1/4 C. + 2 T. water
1/4 tsp. cream of tartar

Boil sugar, water and cream of tartar until amber-colored. Do not stir. It helps to do this in a white porcelain lined pan so that you can see the sugar start to turn. As the edges start turning amber color, take the pan off of the burner and gently rotate pan. It will start to brown all over. You can return the pan to the heat if it needs to brown more. Coat bottom of ramekins.

Custard:
1/4 C. water
1-1/3 C. Half and Half
1/2 C. sugar
2 eggs
4 egg yolks
3 tsp. vanilla

Bring Half and Half, water and sugar to a boil. Gently combine whole eggs, egg yolks and vanilla. Add cooled cream and sugar into eggs in dribbles and stir (do not beat) carefully. Pour through fine sieve and into individual ramekins. Bake in water bath for 30-40 minutes. If a sharp knife comes out clean, the custard is set. Cool and refrigerate until cold. Run a sharp knife around edge and turn over onto a dessert plate to unmold. Gently shake ramekin if the custard does not fall out immediately.

Sautéed Pears:
1/2 stick butter, melted
1/4 C. brown sugar

Melt butter in sauté pan. Add sugar and stir until it melts. Add sliced pears and quickly sauté. Place around crème caramel.

Revolutionary Breakfast

Charleston Brunch

Midwest Farmhand's Lunch

Le Picnique Southwestern Style

The Captain's Table

Revolutionary Breakfast

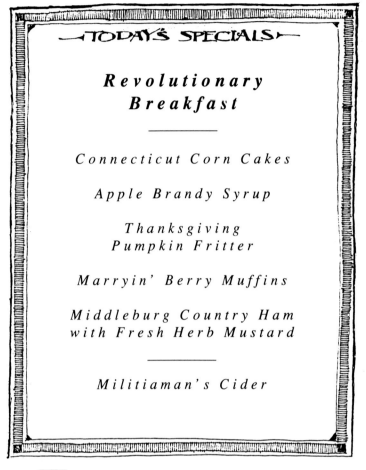

TODAY'S SPECIALS

Revolutionary Breakfast

Connecticut Corn Cakes

Apple Brandy Syrup

Thanksgiving Pumpkin Fritter

Marryin' Berry Muffins

Middleburg Country Ham with Fresh Herb Mustard

Militiaman's Cider

The American revolution in antiques is a 20th century phenomenon. Until 1920, the principal sources of this country's collectors were Western Europe and the Orient. Legend has it that about this time, a resourceful New York dealer pointed at American furniture, detailed and extolled the virtues and said, "Look what you're missing!" The incredible upward spiral of public demand and market price of American antiques that he presumably started continues to make the record books, thanks at least in part to the promotion, persistence and self-fulfilling prophecies of this same dealer's heirs and a few of their competitors. When we Americans get the right idea late, we tend to make up for lost time…sometimes even over-

As you can plainly see, George and Thomas were just here having breakfast before the distant sound of musket fire caused them to run for their horses (leaving coat, boots and gun behind, it seems). Even a small corner of simple, early American furniture moves us to remember our history, enables us to be a part of it and makes us feel "at home" in the 18th century. Some of the American pieces in this set are a bit later, but the mood prevails.

1. *Maple and Cherry Tavern Table, c. 1790;* **2.** *Pine Windsor Chair, c. 1830;* **3.** *Painted Pine Church Pew, c. 1860;* **4.** *Hide-covered Document Box, c. 1820;* **5.** *Copper Eagle from Weathervane, c. 1800;* **6.** *Chippendale Mahogany Mirror, c. 1790;* **7.** *Two 18th C. Charcoal Portraits;* **8.** *Pewter Charger, c. 1790;* **9.** *Patriotic Needlework Picture, c. 1880;* **10.** *Miscellaneous 19th C. Pewter and Iron Umbrella Stand with Walking Sticks, all 19th C.; and* **11.** *a Persian Mat, c. 1920.*

compensate…for past neglect. To some of us, the history of American antiques is a case in point.

As indicated earlier, the broad focus of our antique business has always been the treasures of England, France and America, in that order. Deliberate, but decidedly not unpatriotic, this sequence reflects the interests of our customers, availability and location of sources, personal taste and what we continue to regard as aberrations in the value system of American antiques.

After acknowledging personal preference for Country French furniture, followed closely by Country English; we would still loudly proclaim the American Chippendale highboy — as made in Philadelphia in the late 18th century — as our choice for world-wide, all-time flower of the furniture maker's art. Perhaps there is no price that should be considered too much to pay for a superior Philadelphia highboy, just as there seems to be no ceiling on the works of certain French Impressionists. There are other American classics including, in our opinion, pilgrim chairs and tables, all Blockfront chests and desks, 18th century Windsor chairs and most Federal tester beds that join the highboy as unique American contributions to the history of furniture. The unusually high prices of these classics, compared to English furniture of similar age and quality, may be justified because there is no similar English style. These are American originals. The problem is that one also finds such comparatively high prices (often two to three times more than English counterparts that are actually 20-30 years older and better crafted from finer woods) on most other American furniture — furniture that was made either by English immigrant craftsmen, or their descendents, from English designs. Certainly, there were changes and improvements as each man applied his talents, but essentially, most American furniture and accessories that were made before 1850 were copies, or modifications, of English (or Continental) originals, made by craftsmen who were limited to the tools and materials that were readily available in a new land.

Philadelphia Chippendale Highboy, c. 1780.

After all, frontier life didn't leave much time for designing and developing new and better products. The work of these early craftsmen, from furniture to candlesticks, copies or originals, primitive or fine, constitute a patrimony of which Americans are justifiably proud. Some of the best examples may be priceless. The next echelon has sufficient long-term value to command considerable cash from collectors but the rest...the ordinary...have profited unreasonably from a filter-down effect and are, in our opinion, overpriced by comparison

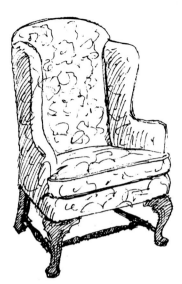

American Queen Anne Wing Chair, c. 1740.

to the European alternatives. Consider, for example, the major antique show with a prime space exhibitor featuring an American table, c. 1790, that has been stripped, refinished, partially re-legged, and shot at, adorned with a carefully typed tag revealing a vague but lengthy provenance and a five figure price. Walk a short distance in either direction to a display of English furniture (same early period) to discover a similar and comparable table in original condition with specific provenance and a price shorter by one digit. Assuming that age, quality and condition are the same, one must suspect that the price of the American table includes a chauvinistic add-on — a large one that a value hunter cannot justify.

There's admittedly some exaggeration here to make the point that one's love for country is not compromised by subjecting American antiques to the same objective standards of quality and price that apply to imports. Even the committed American furniture collectors who would not consider tainting their interiors with foreign furniture owe it to themselves and to their heirs to ask pointed questions about the value they are getting for their money. Those who simply like antiques of a particular period and are not concerned whether the piece is English or American will find that, more often than not, even the finest period imports from the United Kingdom are comparatively good buys in this country.

If all the idiosyncrasies of the marketplace in England, France or the U.S. tell us any one thing, it is that as long as more and more people are more and more able and anxious to buy the static number of real antiques in the world, good things will be harder and harder to find and prices will go higher and higher. If the same idiosyncrasies tell us any other thing, it's that you should be out there hunting and buying...right now!

C o n n e c t i c u t   C o r n   C a k e s

Maize was one of the most prolific crops during early American history and was used in every conceivable way. These corn cakes are the delicious contemporary version of flapjacks.

2 C. boiling water
2 C. yellow corn meal
4 T. bacon grease
2 T. sugar
1-3/4 C. buttermilk
1 C. flour
2 tsp. salt
2 tsp. baking powder
2 eggs

Scald 2 C. water and add to 2 C. yellow corn meal. Let sit for 20 minutes. Add bacon grease and the remaining ingredients and mix until moist. Place scant 1/4 C. batter to hot vegetable oil with a small amount of bacon grease (for flavor) added.

Small versions of these pancakes are delicious as appetizers with homemade chutney, salsa and sour cream as topping.

A p p l e   B r a n d y   S y r u p

Maple syrup was widely used in colonial times. It not only sweetened corn cakes, but helped thicken and flavor stews. The amount of brandy needed in this recipe largely depends on the cook's taste — or inclination.

2 C. maple syrup
2 T. Brandy
1 apple, coarsely chopped
2 T. currants
2 T. pecans

Warm syrup gently and add rest of ingredients. Let this syrup sit for at least one day to marry the flavors.

Thanksgiving Pumpkin Fritters

The taste of a fall harvest permeates these fun fritters. They are a nice change from the traditional pumpkin bread.

3 eggs
1 C. brown sugar
1 C. cooked pumpkin, puréed
4 C. flour
1-1/2 T. shortening
1 tsp. baking soda
2 tsp. baking powder
1/2 tsp. each cinnamon,
   nutmeg, ginger
1/2 tsp. salt

Cream sugar and shortening, beat in 3 eggs, pumpkin and beat well. Stir dry ingredients into egg mixture just until blended together. Drop by full tablespoons into hot oil (360 degrees) until nicely browned. Roll in cinnamon and sugar mixture.

Marryin' Berry Muffins

It is an old rural custom to "marry" two or three kinds of berries into pies and muffins as it makes the fruit flavor more intense.

1/2 C. granulated sugar
1-1/2 C. all purpose flour
2 tsp. baking powder
1/2 tsp. salt
1 tsp. ground cinnamon
1/4 tsp. cloves
1 egg
1 stick butter, melted
1/2 C. Half and Half
1/2 C. raspberries
1/4 C. blueberries
1/4 C. blackberries
Zest of 1 lemon

Streusel Topping:
1/2 C. brown sugar
1/4 C. flour
1/2 C. chopped pecans
1 tsp. cinnamon
2 T. butter, melted

Sift sugar, flour, baking powder, salt, cinnamon and cloves together in a large mixing bowl. Whisk together egg, butter, and Half & Half. Make a well in the center of flour mixture and place egg mixture in the center. Mix together with a spoon just until blended. Carefully stir in berries and zest. Fill each muffin cup 1/2 full and top with streusel topping. Bake at 350 degrees for 20-25 minutes.

Gingered Apple Butter

This butter is fairly spicy with the addition of Calvados and freshly grated ginger. It is wonderful on muffins or with hickory-smoked chicken.

3 lbs. Granny Smith apples —
*   peeled, cored, and chopped*
1 C. apple cider
3/4 C. Calvados
1 C. brown sugar
1 tsp. minced fresh ginger
2 tsp. ground cinnamon
1 tsp. ground allspice
1/8 tsp. freshly grated nutmeg

Place first three ingredients in a heavy saucepan over medium heat for approximately 20 minutes or until apples are tender. Place apple mixture in food processor and purée until smooth. Add the remaining ingredients and process until smooth. Return the apple mixture to the saucepan and simmer for approximately 20-30 minutes more or until it is thick.

Charleston Brunch

TODAY'S SPECIALS

Charleston Brunch

---

*Low Country
Breakfast Shrimp*

Saffron Rice

The Rainbow Row Salad

Benne Seed Biscuits

Zucchini Custard

Sherried Fig Cake

Rum Shrub

Buying American antiques with objectivity means knowing how to recognize the "good stuff" and what it should cost. It's possible to enhance recognition by taking courses or reading books, but the most pleasant and effective way is to spend a few days discovering some of the famous East Coast restorations/re-creations of 17th to 19th century communities. Not only do they enable a trek back in time with fully furnished private and public buildings, workshops and transportation of the period, they also offer the proper regional cuisine, cooked according to the old recipes and served by waiters in period costume to the tune of period songs performed on period instruments. You may choose to have brunch in Charleston between

The food and furniture of the different regions of America are fascinating on-site studies. Antique hunters don't need much encouragement to travel, are more aware than most people of the pleasure of the past and are undoubtedly walking down the streets of Charleston right this minute looking for a proper period place for brunch. Proper, in the South, means equipped with elegant, early American furniture — Queen Anne, Chippendale, Hepplewhite and Sheraton — but with a southern accent!

The young lady in red in the 1. portrait, c. 1800, is questioning how southern these pieces of furniture are, but she knows that the period is right. After all, she's hanging right over 2. a Chippendale Mahogany Flip-top Tea Table, c. 1790, flanked by 3. a pair of 19th C. English pottery urns. 4. A walnut Queen Anne Side Chair, c. 1740, is almost hidden by 5. the Chippendale Mahogany Dropleaf Gateleg Dining Table that is almost hidden by Keitha's scrumptious southern cooking (she lived in Charleston, so she

visits to the superbly appointed 18th century homes in that charming and historic city, or try North Carolina's Old Salem Village for a peek at cottage life in the Old South. Our New England choices are Mystic Seaport in Connecticut and Sturbridge Village in Massachusetts. Whichever one of these "treasures" you choose (and we hope, eventually, you'll choose them all), plan your visit to coincide with one of the major antique shows or flea markets that invariably spring up around such attractions.

If you can find time for only one of these short courses in American history, take three days to really "do" Colonial Williamsburg — Virginia's American classic by which all other restorations are judged — where you can stay in Colonial houses or inns while indulging in the feasts of furniture and food. The superior range and quality of the collections of Abby Aldrich Rockefeller, so effectively displayed in her museum near the Williamsburg Inn, offer an extraordinary opportunity to develop some perspective for judging the folk art scene (more later on this subject).

The period rooms of American furniture housed in major museums across the country are showcases of American craftsmanship. Even though the collections are seldom chronologically complete, they nonetheless train the collector's eye while they entertain. For the full presentation with the finest quality, treat yourself to a day in the new American Wing of the Metropolitan Museum of Art in New York City. Augmenting this unrivaled display of American decorative arts is a gallery of superior surplus that is creatively displayed for the specific benefit of learning lookers. It's difficult to imagine how a year with text books could be as helpful to a serious student of American antiques as eight hours in this gallery (and the mid-day break can include a serious study of Country French cuisine at Le Refuge, just a couple of blocks east of the Met's front door).

The famous Garvan collection at Yale University affords another training treat. The magnitude and magnificence of this splendid private collection together with the ingenious method of display provide a particularly effective focus on American furniture. Speaking of such things as magnitude and magnificence leads us to the subject of Winterthur, the Wilmington, Delaware landmark residence of Henry Francis DuPont, that houses his definitive private collection of American art and antiques. Winterthur offers an hour tour of highlights or several longer (by reservation) tours of the major collections. Manage an in-depth tour if possible, particularly if you are

knows what she's cooking about!)

The accessories are pressed glass, silverplate and porcelain of no great age or significance, but the arrangement of fresh fruit is a contemporary work of art which you can create by following the clear and concise directions on page 32.

American Chippendale Drop-front Desk, c. 1780.

*American Federal (Hepple-
white) Side Chair, c. 1790.*

devoted to American Federal furniture. Stay the night in the Brandywine Valley, dine in nearby Kennett Square, Pennsylvania (the mushroom capital of the world, according to the ads) and take a morning to visit the fabulous gardens of Longwood — another treasure provided by the DuPonts.

Unfortunately, museums do not indicate a current market value on their collections, so there's more research for you to do…in shops, perusing auction catalogues and attending sales (especially the ones in New York and New England), studying price books that indicate age and condition as well as listing a value, and poking around estate sales and flea markets. As indicated earlier, the more "hands on" experience you can get, the better. The ads which appear in trade publications are helpful as you can test your eye by trying to determine the age and origin of the piece in the photo before checking the fine-print description. Prices are seldom included in ads, but a call to the owner should provide that and other useful information. In our opinion (which is shared by many, many dealers and collectors) the *Maine Antique Digest* (known as 'M.A.D.') is the most useful publication for both neophyte and advanced collectors of Americana. The coverage of shows and auctions which this publication provides includes a surprising amount of price information and gives an insider's view which is so incisive and informative that reading about the event is almost better than being there.

Now, try your well-trained eye and new-found expertise on a flea market. Anywhere will do, but for early Americana, the further east you go the better your chances for discovery will be. Bet a little money on your judgment — it's a quick way to find out how much you know and it will increase your incentive to learn more. The fascination

of hunting antiques is that you can never learn quite all you need to know about them…the more you hunt, the more you realize how much more you need to learn!

Low Country Breakfast Shrimp

Buying shrimp from a Shem Creek Trawler is fascinating and the shrimp are unbelievably good. This brunch dish is a must for that "Low Country" taste. While this version is rather mild, it can be made spicier with the addition of cayenne pepper.

6 slices bacon
1/2 C. chopped green onion
1/4 C. chopped green and
    red pepper
3 — 4 C. peeled and deveined
    raw shrimp
2 T. Worcestershire Sauce
1/4 C. tomato paste
3 T. flour
2 C. water, hot
dash tabasco
2 cloves garlic, minced

Saffron Rice:

2 C. brown rice
4 C. chicken stock
1 tsp. saffron
1/2 C. chopped onions
1/2 C. chopped celery
cayenne pepper

Sauté bacon, green onions, peppers until crisp — tender — add shrimp and quickly sauté until they have just turned pink. Add 1-1/2 C. water. Simmer 5 minutes and thicken with flour and water mixture. Add Worcestershire and tomato paste. Cook slowly until the sauce thickens. Serve with Saffron Rice — tossed with green onion and celery.

Saffron Rice — combine rice, chicken stock, saffron and sautéed vegetables in 9" x 12" baking dish. Bake for 1 hour at 350 degrees. Sauté in butter: chopped onions, chopped celery, cayenne pepper.

Zucchini Custard

Vegetable custards of all kinds are served in the South. The flavor can be varied by simply substituting cheddar with dried mustard and fresh herb seasoning.

2 T. butter
3 T. green onion, chopped
4 — 6 zucchini, shredded
1 C. cream
2 eggs
1/4 tsp. nutmeg
salt & pepper
3/4 C. Gruyere cheese
Parmesan cheese

Sauté onion and zucchini in butter until transparent. Drain in a colander. Mix eggs, cream, spices, cheese and zucchini together. Pour mixture into a well-buttered soufflé dish that has been dusted with Parmesan cheese. Bake at 350 degrees for 30 minutes or until custard is set.

Benne Seed Biscuits

Benne Seeds are used in traditional Charleston recipes of cocktail wafers, biscuits, brittle, and cookies. They were brought to this country by slaves and are said to bring good luck to anyone who eats or plants them.

2 C. flour
2 T. sugar
1-1/2 T. baking powder
1/2 tsp. cream of tartar
1/4 tsp. salt
1/2 C. butter, cut into pieces
2/3 C. whipping cream
4 T. benne seeds or
  sesame seeds

Sift flour, sugar, baking powder, cream of tartar and salt. Cut in butter until it resembles coarse meal. Add cream and seeds. Stir until just incorporated. Knead gently on lightly floured board. Cut into desired shape and dip in melted butter. Bake at 400 degrees for 15 minutes, brush tops with butter and sprinkle seeds on top.

Sherried Fig Cake

Sherried Fig Cake is a very rich tea cake made for centuries by fine cooks in Charleston. Use sherry liberally.

1 C. butter
3 C. sugar
5 eggs
3-1/2 C. flour
3/4 C. milk
1-1/2 tsp. baking powder
2 tsp. vanilla
1/2 C. water

Cream butter with 2 C. sugar, add eggs one at a time, beating thoroughly after each addition. Sift dry ingredients together and add alternately with milk. Bake in two 9" greased cake pans at 350 degrees for 40 minutes. Make a syrup of 1 C. sugar, 1/4 C. water, 1/4 C. sherry. Add vanilla spread over the layer after you remove them from the pans.

Icing for Sherried Fig Cake:
2 C. raisins
2 C. pecans
1 C. chopped figs
1/4 C. sherry
2 C. sugar
2/3 C. water
2 tsp. corn syrup
2 egg whites, beaten until stiff

Soak figs, pecans and raisins in 1/4 C. sherry. Cook water, sugar, corn syrup to a soft-ball stage. Gradually pour into 2 stiffly beaten egg whites. Fold in pecans, figs, and raisins. Spread between layers and on top and sides of cake.

Midwest Farmhand's Lunch

―TODAY'S SPECIALS―

Midwest Farmhand's Lunch

Cider-Glazed Missouri Country Ham

Peppered Smoked Turkey

Great Plains Slaw

Sour Cream Potatoes

Patch Tomatoes with Red Onions

Tom's Confetti Salad

Pauls Valley Pecan & Chocolate Pie

Grandma's Chocolate Pound Cake

When you're next invited to an 'honest-to-good-ness-down-home farmhands' brunch at the old Midwestern homestead of an antique collector, you can expect to be entertained in a proper country setting, complete with folk art and early furniture — and you might not be disappointed. Certainly the ingredients are available — though the term "folk art" may be interpreted even more liberally in the Midwest than in the East — and the term "early" for regional furniture means circa 1840 and later.

Folk art is another one of those anamolies that keep popping up in the hunt for American antiques. While the term has been used for generations by Americans with reference to the traditional or tribal arts and crafts of

foreign countries, the popular application to American antiques is of recent origin and much less specific. The promotion of American folk art as an important collecting possibility seems to have started in the mid-1900s with the publication of several anthologies of American design. These books displayed in compelling color the hand-crafted creations of two-plus centuries — from wine glasses to water buckets. To the previous recognition of primitive art in America was suddenly added a boundless enthusiasm for the primitive crafts…the quilts and carvings, signs and saddles…toys and tables and a thousand other decorative/useful things, made by hand from original designs, usually anonymously. With fine early American furniture already beyond the financial reach of most collectors, folk art found a quick response — which, in turn, triggered a quick rise in prices. The tale of the duck decoy, made in 1930 (sale price $1.50), discovered in 1970 by antiquers (sale price $45.00), auctioned in 1985 (sale price $65,000) is not exaggerated and is not isolated. The latest auction record for a duck decoy is a stout $319,000!

Similar trends developed in connection with ordinary farm weather vanes, whirley-gigs, ship models, whaling paraphenalia, goose, shorebird and fish decoys, quilts and rugs, cigar-store Indians and barber poles. The list goes on...and the price goes up. Specialist dealers began appearing at antique shows with no more than ten pieces of folk art, dramatically displayed, expensively lighted and extravagantly priced. The difficulties of achieving similarly artful in-home displays of eight-foot-tall rooster weathervanes or 500-pound carousel horses were overcome by room additions entirely devoted to such eccentricities. And a new generation of collectors was born...a wealthy new generation. By the time the American Country look came along a few years later, folk art originals had followed 18th century furniture upwards to a price level out of the reach of most potential buyers. To answer the new demand for "Country" interiors, the definition of folk art was extended considerably — first to anything that was hand-crafted, whether well-designed and executed or not, then to anything that was uniquely American — whether hand-crafted or not.

Overnight, collectibles became antiques in the minds of both buyers and sellers. Many so-called "antique price guides" went along with the popular trend and chronicled high prices on an endless variety of mass-produced junk — as long as it was mass produced in America. The latest development in folk art is the production of overt copies of 18th and 19th century pieces. Some of these are finely crafted by hand from original designs...here in America...and find a temporary home in elegant shops at high prices. (Most are properly attributed

liquor sign, a framed metal saddlery sign, c. 1890, a zinc horse head sign for Omaha tack shop, c. 1900, and a glamorous 2-sided sheet metal harness sign, c. 1880; **9.** *Some team harness, a wood whisky barrel, a pair of English Wood-twist Candlesticks and a pottery jug, all c. 1900, complete the picture of nostalgia.*

American Carved Wood Eagle Finial, c. 1800.

Flea Market Folk Art

There are still opportunities to discover real American folk art at reasonable prices, especially at regional flea markets. Midwest hunters invariably find some "pretty good" decoys, handmade quilts, tramp art and weather-vanes.

Some early, handmade charmers that have not caught on yet and are still cheap are lace, children's clothes, shellcrafts and Victorian beadwork in all shapes and sizes.

to contemporary artisans, some are not.) Other copies are machine-made in foreign lands and find their temporary shelter in discount stores. Are these, too, folk art? Where do we go for the next batch?

There is undeniable appeal to the pieces that were selected for the design anthologies. They have important things to say about the history, culture and personality of this country and its people. Fortunately, many of the finer pieces made it to museums and are available for all to see and enjoy. Still, we face an obvious dilemma in attempting to place realistic values on American treasures when a duck decoy that is only partially hand-crafted and only 50 years old sells for six figures — approximately the value of our entire inventory of 18th and early 19th century English and French antiques.

It's discouraging to attend "antique" flea markets and fairs across the country and have to sort through the endless attic, basement and barn accumulations of used toys, tools, plates, clothes, harness and gate hinges that are included at absurdly high prices because some buyers' guide lists them under "American antiques and folk art." They are neither. Fortunately, among all the trivia, there are often some very good pieces of early, handmade European antiques that are quite inexpensive because they are not listed in "the book" and therefore not recognized for what they are by their current owners. There are also some nice, but still neglected, pieces of American hand-crafts — folk art for you to discover.

In summary, it seems obvious from out here in the Midlands that hunters of American folk art and collectors of any other American antiques need to be concerned about the long-term value they're getting for monies spent in today's volatile and sometimes whimsical American market. A little chauvinistic value is okay. A lot is not. To

avoid coming home with a sack full (or a house full) of "the king's new clothes," you only need to apply the same standards of objectivity with regard to age, quality, condition and price when you buy American "antiques" that make such good sense when you buy those from England, France or any place else. It is not unAmerican to do so, and it can be financially disastrous to do anything else.

Cider-Glazed Missouri Country Ham

Missouri produces some wonderful country hams that make great hors d'oeurves with zucchini biscuits. Or try this fabulous Harvest Sandwich that we serve in Le Picnique.

Country ham, salt cured
2 gallons apple cider
1 gallon water
2 or 3 apples, coarsely cut
1 T. whole cloves

Soak ham for 2 hours in clear water, rinse and change water again. This time add 1 gallon of apple cider to 1 gallon of water and pour over ham. Simmer for 2 hours. Rinse ham again and this time put in large roaster with 1 gallon cider, 2 or 3 coarsely cut apples, 1 tablespoon whole cloves and bake at 325 degrees. Baste every 30 minutes with liquid from pan.

Harvest Sandwiches:
Pumpernickel bread
Raspberry mustard
Arugula
Sliced medium Cheddar cheese
Country ham

Spread pumpernickel bread slices with raspberry mustard (1 C. mustard with 1/2 C. raspberries). Top with arugula, country ham and sliced medium sharp Cheddar cheese. Broil open-faced until cheese has melted and ham is warm.

Great Plains Slaw

This Great Plains Slaw is a very popular side dish made in Le Picnique. It needs to be tossed together right before serving or the cabbage wilts.

1 head red cabbage
1 lb. bacon
1/2 C. walnuts
2 T. butter
1/2 tsp. rosemary

Julienne 1 head of red cabbage. Brown 1 lb. bacon, drain and crumble. Sauté walnuts in butter and rosemary. Toss all with vinaigrette.

Balsamic Vinaigrette:
1 C. olive oil
1/3 C. salad oil
1/4 C. red wine vinegar
2 cloves minced garlic
6 oz. Dijon mustard
2 eggs, beaten
ground pepper

Whisk together and pour over cabbage, bacon and walnut mixture.

Sour Cream Potatoes

Just the aroma from these potatoes will make guests or family anxious for dinner. They are truly addictive!

1 pint sour cream
1/2 pint cream
2 cloves garlic, minced
salt & pepper
1 C. shredded Swiss cheese
1/2 C. Parmesan cheese
pinch nutmeg
baking potatoes, peeled, sliced into even 1/8" slices

Lightly oil glass baking dish. Mix sour cream, cream, garlic, salt, pepper and pinch nutmeg. Dip potato slices in mixture and line slices upright in parallel lines in baking dish. Pour remaining sauce over the potatoes until covered. Seal tightly with foil and bake at 350 degrees for 1 hour or until potatoes are fork tender. Sprinkle cheese over top and let melt —10 minutes. They must be tightly covered as the sauce will get too brown and the potatoes will become dry.

Grandma's Chocolate Pound Cake

This cake recipe predates the Civil War. Can you imagine trying to make this without a mixer? It is one of those cakes that is better a day after it is baked and freezes beautifully.

1 lb. butter
3 C. sugar
5 eggs
3 C. flour
4 rounded T. of cocoa
1 C. milk
2 tsp. vanilla
2 tsp. baking powder
1 tsp. salt

Cream butter and sugar together, then beat in eggs one at a time. Sift dry ingredients together and add alternately with milk and vanilla. Bake 1 hour at 350 degrees in well-oiled and floured tube pan. Let cool inverted.

Le Picnique Southwestern Style

—TODAY'S SPECIALS—

Le Picnique
Southwestern Style

————

Seafood Skewer with
Cilantro Butter

Desert Rice

Keitha's
Corn Chowder

Tucson Black Beans

Chocolate Border Cake

Compared to the vastness of the territory, the differences in early 19th century regional furniture in the western two-thirds of America are surprisingly small. The early pioneers might have enjoyed a Southwestern picnic spread upon the same kind of long pine table with plank top and square tapered or turned legs that would have accommodated a Midwestern brunch. Seating would have been similar too — ladder-back or bentwood chairs — maybe trestle benches, all of native woods with a frontier personality. Wardrobes, pie safes, blanket chests and step-back cupboards made in places that are 2,000 miles apart will differ only in carved or painted decoration influenced by the local European immigrants or by proximity to

It has to be exciting country where the influences of Colonial Mexico, American Indians, the old frontier and the new California wine industry all come together. Certainly many of today's most popular food concepts... served around the world... are based on southwestern cuisine...and accompanied by large side orders of Napa Valley Chardonnay. One of our all-time favorite categories of antiques — the wood carved Santos — are indigenous to the area, and while expensive to the purchaser, are appealing enough to be worth the investment risk.

Our southwestern picnique is served on 1. an impressive long pine settle with simple chip-carved decoration, c. 1870, lighted by and 2. an early 19th C. Mexican Tole Candlestick, standing on 3. an exceptionally decorative, small Indian Mat, c. 1920. Standing over the feast is 4. a superb Santo, a carved and poly-chromed figure of St. Joseph, c. 1780, from Portuguese Goa. His platform is 5. an iron-bound, copper-clad Arts & Crafts Treasure Chest,

colonial Mexico.

The territorial sameness that extends to the antiques produced west of Pittsburgh, however, does not extend to the collectors. Cross a threshold today in such disparate destinations as Indianapolis, Baton Rouge, Fort Worth, St. Paul, Tucson or Seattle and find treasures from all over the world, personally imported by their globe-trotting owners from equally disparate places...London, Paris, Rome, Hong Kong, New York, Savannah and Old Lyme. Most of the importing was done pre-World War II when the private buyer had a large choice of choice pieces. The result is that estate sales/auctions in the contiguous states west of the Alleghenies are as likely to produce antique treasures as those held in states closer to the Atlantic seaboard — perhaps not in such concentration...but still in quantities worthy of a serious hunt... with prices that are a major travel incentive.

Because the antique interest in this locale is focused on Americana, the best buys are European furniture and decorations, Oriental porcelain and rugs. It's astonishing to observe the frenzy that follows the announcement of a sale with significant 18th and early 19th century American furniture, no matter how inaccessible the site. Phone lines are clogged, tiny regional airports scramble to handle the traffic from points east and the determination of those seeking early access to the merchandise can only be described as murderous. The chance of lower prices on Americana are sufficient to draw dealers half-way across the country. In our view, the possible buys on good, early English and French are even better. (A further unbiased observation is that antique prices in Midland shops are also much lower than one finds on either coast.) There are so many fine Oriental rugs in the Midwest that dealers come from all over to buy locally and sell internationally. Even minor estate sales will include Orientals; often extremely rare ones.

Where do you go to find these treasures? It's useless to deny the envy outlanders feel for the collectors on the East Coast who can choose which of seven major auctions they only have to go across town to attend each week...or which of several hundred weekend shows, fairs, country auctions and flea markets they can reach in a half-day journey. Still, there is happy hunting in the Heartland — it just takes more patience and effort. Liquidation of worldly goods is sometimes accomplished through an auction, but more frequently the goods are sold at an advertised public sale lasting two or three days. Such *Estate Sales* are priced and managed by private individuals or antique dealers. Prices are usually firm the first day of the sale and negotiable thereafter. Because these estates will include all personal property not claimed by heirs — paintings, furniture, silver, porcelain, crystal, jewelry,

c. 1890; **6.** *the Grape Press and* **7.** *the Iron and Wood Wine Rack are vintage 1930; Keitha's fabulous hot and spicy Corn Chowder is nestled inside* **8.** *a 19th C. southwestern Cheese Drainer;* **9.** *The Tripod Chopping Block, c. 1880, is holding* **10.** *a hide-covered Basket, c. 1900, that might be North Woods, but probably is North African; the Baskets hanging are definitely the newer and older handcrafts of native Americans.*

American Windsor Side Chair, c. 1760.

American Sheraton "fancy" Side Chair, c. 1818.

furs, cars, rugs, toys, clothes and all household equipment — it's difficult to find a manager who can correctly recognize and price such variety while making sure that the property sells. Therefore, there are always good buys for savvy collectors in such sales. The same opportunities exist to a lesser extent in the mass of weekend moving and garage sales.

Auctions, estate sales and garage sales are advertised in the classified section of the local daily papers. Important ones make the big city journals and the regional "antiques" publications. You can track down the flea markets the same way, though with less hope for successful hunting. Real antiques are not plentiful in either the flea markets or the local "antiques centers". Those that sneak in will be fully priced (according to "the book") or hidden under a pile of tomatoes near the comic books. If you're looking for bargains in early porcelain, avoid the dealer who specializes in the same and who will recognize and know the value of his or her inventory. Look instead at the table top of the lace-and-linens-lady who may have had to buy some porcelain in the box with the clothes and wants to unload it. This rule applies generally to the hunt for antiques: the best buys will not be with the specialist (but the best pieces may be). It's always fair in a flea market or estate sale to ask for a better price. The worst the dealer can do is say, "No", and that doesn't happen very often.

We mention these procedures for hunting antiques in the Midwest, Southwest, Northwest and West Coast...not because they're much different from those in the Northeast and Southeast...but because so many folks seem to assume that American antique hunting country is divided into two parts — the East and the rest — and that there's not much worth hunting in the rest. Actually, antiques started west a long time ago, and we've had time

to grow some of our own in the last 150 years. There are even Midwestern restaurants with creative regional cookery that are far ahead of their time. "Homemade meatloaf with cornbread, mashed potatoes and gravy" just made it to the trendy New York restaurants, but it's been on the menu at the local corner café for 60 years. The French that came down the Missouri River left a lot of their recipes too, so get on your horse, or in your boat or your jet plane and come on out for the hunt!

Hunter's Alert!

Large quantities of American Victorian furniture languish in the Midwest, for lack of local interest. Familiarity has bred such contempt that few dealers want to handle it, leaving important Victorian revival and "Lincolnesque" pieces to pass from owner to owner at close-out prices in estate and moving sales. What an opportunity for some resourceful hunter!

American Victorian Rococo Center Hall Table, c. 1850.

Keitha's Corn Chowder

Our corn chowder recipe took top creative cooking award at our local Gourmet Gala and is a regular on our menu during the winter months at Le Picnique.

*1/2 lb. bacon, coarsely
    chopped*
1 onion, finely chopped
*1 red pepper, coarsely
    chopped*
*1 green pepper, coarsely
    chopped*
2+ lb. butter
6 C. frozen corn
2 C. ham, diced
*4 potatoes, peeled and
    chopped*
1/4 C. jalapeno, chopped
*2 C. Half and Half or
    whipping cream*

Sauté bacon, onions, and pepper in 2 lb. butter. Add 4 C. corn, 2 C. ham, 4 chopped potatoes and cover all ingredients with water. Simmer for 1 hour. Purée 2 C. corn with 1 C. cream in food processor and add to the simmering mixture. Cook 30 minutes maximum. Let cool to room temperature and add 2 C. of cream or Half and Half. Add salt, pepper, and jalapenos when rewarming.

Seafood Skewer

Seafood skewers take very little time on the grill and are wonderful either basted with this butter or a nice spicy ginger sauce. Smaller skewers are excellent for appetizers. (If you are using wooden skewers be sure to soak them in water to prevent them from burning.)

*1 lb. shrimp (approx.), peeled
    and deveined*
1/2 lb. scallops
1/2 lb. monk fish, cut into chunks
1/2 lb. fresh tuna, cut into chunks
*1 red onion, cut into
    bite size pieces*
*red and green peppers, cut into
    bite size pieces*
1 lb. mushrooms

Alternate fish chunks with onion and red and green peppers on skewers. Marinate for at least one hour in cilantro marinade. Grill over medium coals toasting and turning every 5 minutes or until done. Brush with cilantro lime butter (following page) just before serving.

Cilantro Marinade — 1 C. fresh lime juice, 2 C. olive oil, 1 bunch chopped cilantro, salt and pepper, 2 cloves minced garlic.

Cilantro Lime Butter — 2 cloves garlic, 1 C. fresh cilantro, salt and pepper, 1 lb. butter, 1 tablespoon fresh lime zest, 2 tablespoons lime juice. Process until smooth. Keep in refrigerator.

T u c s o n   B l a c k   B e a n s

These beans are full of the robust flavors that are synonymous with Southwestern cuisine. It keeps refrigerated indefinitely and is great puréed as a dip for tortilla chips.

1 lb. dried black beans
2 cloves garlic
1/4 C. balsamic vinegar
2/3 C. good olive oil
salt & pepper
juice of 2 lemons, 1 lime
1 large red pepper, finely
*   chopped*
6 scallions, thinly sliced
1/4 C. chopped cilantro

Wash beans and place in a pan. Cover with water and place on high heat to boil. Boil for 5 minutes and turn off heat and let stand for 1 hour. Drain and remove beans and again cover with water and a few sprigs of cilantro and 1 clove of garlic. Simmer until tender, about 1 hour. Drain and rinse beans and toss with pepper, scallions, and chopped cilantro. Mix together other ingredients and pour over beans. Cover and let stand at least 4 hours.

The Captain's Table

TODAY'S SPECIALS

The Captain's Table

---

*Summer
Artichoke Soup*

Shore Salad

Portsmouth Potatoes

Cape Corn Salad

Garlic French Bread

*Fresh
Raspberry Tartlets*

Even if your hunting territory is limited to the United States, by choice or necessity, you still have the treasures of the world to choose from…in so many exciting places. Fortunately, some of the most appealing cultural and gastronomic destinations also offer the best antiquing. New York City has to top the list with the most choices of places to go and things to buy when you get there…whether antiques or meals are the objects of the search. The infinite number of restaurants, shops and galleries plus the major auction houses in the nation present a rare opportunity to find anything from anywhere at any price. Paradoxically, it's all those choices and the impossibility of covering them that make the chase in New

Professional accessories such as lobster traps and trap markers (all color coded to identify the trapper) cost so little and have so much appeal that we like to use them with antiques. Ex-ship equipment is a popular "almost antique" category in New England...and in old England also. While most of it is not handmade, some ship's wheels and instruments can cost more than period tables. Legitimate ship and shore antiques are many, of course: decoys, ship models and the fascinating half-hull models used to design ships can range in price from absurdly high to bargain-of-the-year.

Our lobster supper was cooked in these English copper pans, 1. a stock pot, c. 1860 and 2. a bradded sauce pan, c. 1830, by the light of 3. this pair of 19th century ship's lanterns. It is served on 4. a table made from a 17th century iron-bound Hatch Cover on a handsome, handmade wrought-iron base.

"Oakwood" is the name of 5. the 3-masted 19th century copper Weathervane complete with original pole.

York so frustrating. San Francisco and New Orleans offer similar quality but less quantity in a smaller, friendlier space. Los Angeles and Dallas complete our list of favorite shopping cities...we have good luck hunting in each of these five cities so we return often, but we know there are other cities with which we are not so familiar that also have much to offer. Regionally, New England has no peer...antiques are a way of life there...and the bounty from the sea gives even an ordinary roadside café an unfair edge in the national food competition. With a couple of weeks to explore, planned around country inn accommodations and M.A.D.'s monthly calendar of sales, fairs and auctions, the intrepid collector could cover Boston, Cape Cod, Nantucket, Martha's Vineyard and selected points in

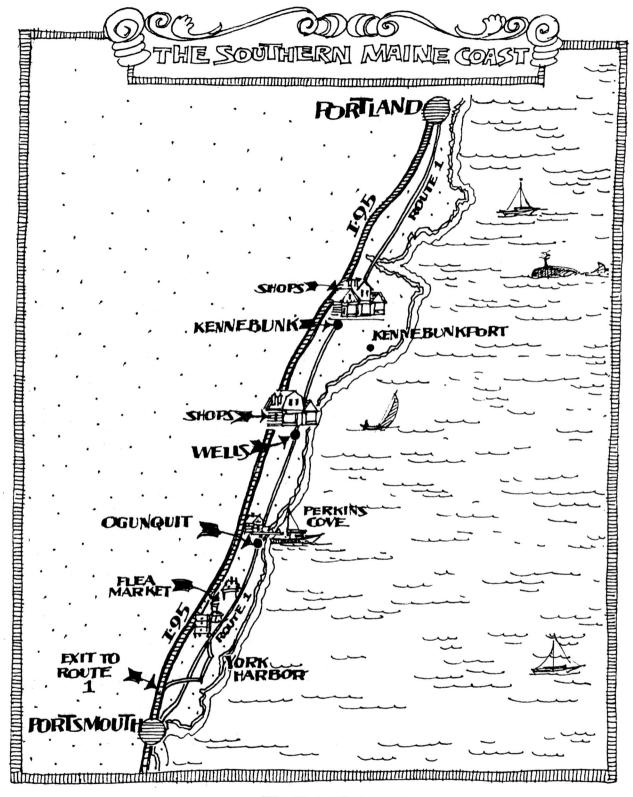

TREASURES

The Southern Maine Coast — 1 - 1-1/2 Hours North of Boston

American Transitional Queen Anne/Chippendale Side Chair, c. 1760.

Vermont, New Hampshire and Maine. Given only a couple of days, you must spend them on the southern coast of Maine — partly because of the spectacular scenery, partly because of the limitless antiquing possibilities and partly because of the lobster lunches, dinners and shore snacks. We are so captivated by the charms of this area that we have used Boston as a gateway to Europe on buying trips so as to take advantage of the 4- to 5-hour layover for a quick foray up the coast.

Follow the signs to I-95 North from Logan Airport — and just beyond Portsmouth take the York Beach exit to Highway 1. You begin to see small shops and roadside antique markets almost immediately. Watch for the Perkins Cove turn sign in the center of Ogunquit so you can make a quick detour to one of the most delightful tiny fishing villages in the world — and a good place to take a lobstering cruise. There are some shops on the wharf but the antiquing really picks up as you continue north toward Wells. Go ahead and stop at every antique sign so you can work up an appetite for a two-for-the-price-of-one lobster lunch in Wells or on the road out to Wells Beach. On the north edge of the village is an antique center worth a couple of hours time at least (you can get a list of Route 1 shops from any dealer). Perhaps it's time to go back to a waterside inn in Ogunquit to rest up for the journey on up to Kennebunk. It's not far, but the trip could take you most of a day if you take the side roads to all of the shops and cover the markets the way you should. Find a place on the water and eat some more lobster in Kennebunkport before heading back to Boston with the magic treasures of New England, many of which were free and yours for the memory. Maine in winter undoubtedly has a different face, but in late spring, summer or early fall, this little trip is a treasure!

Cape Corn Salad

This corn salad is refreshing and a great picnic food. It must be made with fresh corn for that delicious flavor and crispness.

1/4 C. lemon juice
1/4 C. tarragon vinegar
1 minced garlic clove
1 tsp. salt
1/4 freshly ground pepper
1 T. sugar
1-1/2 salad oil
1/4 C. jalapeno pepper, chopped
16 ears fresh corn, cooked and kernels cut off (must be fresh)
1 red pepper, coarsely chopped
1 green pepper, coarsely chopped
6 green onions, coarsely chopped

Mix first 8 ingredients and pour over corn, peppers and onions. Let marinate several hours.

Summer Artichoke Soup

The addition of sour cream and caviar makes this recipe incredibly rich. We sometimes serve it from a demitasse cup before summer dinner parties.

4 C. fresh artichoke hearts
4 T. butter
1/4 C. onion
4 C. chicken stock, well seasoned
1 garlic clove
1 C. whipping cream
salt & white pepper
1/4 tsp. nutmeg
sour cream and caviar
juice from 1 lemon

Sauté onion and garlic in butter. Add artichoke hearts, stock and seasonings. Cook 30 minutes, purée in food processor. Cool. Add cream and adjust seasoning. Serve cold. Top with dollop of sour cream and caviar.

Shore Salad

Fresh lobster has a wonderful nautical flavor, but in deference to buffet guests, it is much easier as a salad. Fresh shrimp may also be added.

6 whole Maine lobsters,
*   water to cover*

Court bouillon:
Salt
Peppercorns
Bay leaves
2 whole lemons
2 garlic cloves, minced
4 gallons water

Place lobsters in boiling court bouillon until shell turns bright red. Their heads must be placed in the water first. Cool and remove meat from the tail and claws.

Salad — lobster meat, 1 C. chopped celery, 1 can of water chestnuts (5 oz.) drained and chopped finely, 2 T. minced green onion, 2 T. caper, 1/2-1 C. mayonnaise, 1-2 teaspoons horseradish, salt and pepper, and lemon juice from one lemon.

Raspberry Tartlets

Early spring raspberries make the perfect fruit tart. The crust is almost a cookie in itself.

Nut Shell Pastry:
8 oz. finely chopped almonds
2-1/2 oz. butter cookie crumbs
1/4 C. sugar
3 C. flour
1 egg, beaten
1 tsp. almond extract

Spray tart pans with vegetable oil. Mix all together and fill six 5" tart pans. Chill for 1 hour. Bake at 350 degrees for 15-20 minutes.

Crème Patisserie:
(See index for recipe but use
vanilla as the flavoring.)
Fresh raspberries

Fill cooled and baked pastry shell with crème patisserie. Top with fresh berries and then brush with apricot glaze.

Apricot Glaze:
1 — 8 oz. jar of apricot jelly
2 T. sugar
1 T. rum

Heat jelly, sugar and rum until boiling. Strain and use to coat pastry shells and tops of fruit tarts.

Postscript

The only place to end a dissertation on two of the world's most popular topics, antiques and food, spanning four centuries, and three countries on two continents (and one island) is where the publishers tell you to quit. So may we end with our best wishes for your good hunting and **some personal thoughts on buying antiques.**

For investment — Recognize that the sure return on your investment in an antique lies in the additional pleasure you will receive through living with a piece of history. Collectors buy to keep, not to sell...but with the confidence that, should they need to sell, they have a far better chance of getting their money out of antiques than out of new furniture or accessories and a reasonable chance of making a profit, depending on elapsed time and market conditions.

To furnish a home — Buy the antiques that you fall in love with and cannot live without...then find a place to put them. Avoid buying to fit a specific place...far better to leave it temporarily vacant than to fill the space with a compromise. Avoid buying to match the color of other furniture...a well integrated mix is more interesting and allows more freedom of selection. Start each room with one major antique piece that you plan to keep forever...no matter where you live...and develop the room around it.

To furnish an office — Antiques...furnishings or accessories or both...provide an office with character and distinction just as they do a home...and there can be significant financial advantages to such a collection. Ask your accountant for further information.

If you're a perfectionist — Recognize that to be an antique, the piece must be quite old, and will inevitably show some indication of that age (use extreme caution in buying it if it does not) which is now part of the character and personality of the piece. While you should not accept a piece in bad structural condition or with shoddy repairs, you cannot expect antiques to look new.

Now that you are a "professional" hunter — You may question the need of continuing to buy in retail shops. Just as good cooks are the most ardent supporters of good restaurants, so the most experienced antique hunters are the best customers of fine retail shops — for these compelling reasons:

• The piece you really want may be there! The professional usually has more time and sources to find the rare and wonderful antiques.

• You get a guarantee that what you pay for is what you get! Even with your sharpened eye, detecting the increasingly prevalent fix-ups and phonies may be difficult and time-consuming.

• You can change your mind! Most shops will let you try major purchases in your home or office before you're committed to buy.

• The retail price may be a bargain! Compared to the compulsive and competitive results of today's auctions and estate sales, shop prices are often more reasonable. If past is truly prologue, even a higher price paid for the piece you prefer to live with will be a good investment today and a bargain tomorrow.

Recipe Index